INTRODUCING BUDDHISM

$9.50

INTRODUCING BUDDHISM

REVISED EDITION

by

KODO MATSUNAMI

CHARLES E. TUTTLE COMPANY
Rutland, Vermont & Tokyo, Japan

Representatives

Continental Europe: PROOST & BRANDT DISTRIBUTION BV, *The Netherlands*

British Isles: SIMON & SCHUSTER INTERNATIONAL GROUP, *London*

Australasia: BOOKWISE INTERNATIONAL
1 Jeanes Street, Beverley, 5009, South Australia

This edition is published by the Charles E. Tuttle Company, Inc.
of Rutland, Vermont & Tokyo, Japan
with editorial offices at
Suido 1-chome, 2-6, Bunkyo-ku, Tokyo, Japan

All rights reserved by Kodo Matsunami

Library of Congress Catalog Card No. 75-28970

International Standard Book No. 0-8048-1192-x

First edition, February, 1965
Second edition, 1966
Revised edition, 1973
Fourth edition, 1976
First Tuttle edition, 1976
Fourth printing, 1987

This book is dedicated
to
the Pioneers of Buddhism
in the West

Contents

Preface to the Revised Edition

This little book does not attempt to give an exposition of any particular thought from the authoritative standpoint of view. It is, on the other hand, a collection of essays on Buddhism which are understood by a Japanese student who sets out for a journey in search of his true self.

Although there are many English books on Buddhism which are written by the Eastern and Western scholars, they are rather difficult to read by the general public, and are sometimes misleading from the Buddhist point of view. It was my long cherished hope to write a comprehensive book on Buddhism from within, so that the readers may understand the accurate form of Buddhism as it existed, and is existing today. It is an undeniable fact that Buddhism still remains in a showbox to be displayed. It is often regarded by Westerners as nothing but one of the exotic religions of the Orient, and real interest in it is only seen in the academic fields in the West.

The time has come for us to think of Buddhism not in terms of temples old and new, or of traditional rituals, but in terms of injecting more vitality to make Buddhism more meaningful to all of us. We of this generation must make it known to the world that Buddhism has a living

significance as a great world religion and can contribute
to the enrichment of world culture.

When I heard of the coming of the 800th Anniversary
of the founding of the Jodo denomination of Buddhism in
1974, I felt more than anything else the pressing need to
introduce some important Buddhist ideas so that this anniversary might become a memorable and meaningful
one for us and for the introduction of Buddhism to the
West. Only for this reason is this book written, and no
other.

My deepest appreciation is given to the students of our
English Seminar who have extended their helping hands
in reading and typing articles. I must also acknowledge
my thankfulness to Miss Bessie Tsuji and Miss Anthea
Haslgrave for their assistance in proofreading my articles
in the last stretch. Without their assistance and cooperation this book would never have been possible.

The Author
February, 1973
Honolulu, Hawaii
U.S.A.

PART I

BUDDHISM IN THOUGHT

Chapter 1

What is Buddhism?

Many people in the past have raised the question, "What is Buddhism?" Innumerable answers and definitions have been given by various scholars, ministers and devotees who interpreted Buddhism in their own way. However, Buddhism is, to me, the guiding light which leads us to know what we really are and what our surroundings are. This insight naturally gives us some orientation when we confront and solve our personal problems which arise out of our surroundings. Here, the inquiries into the existence of God or the after-life are of secondary importance. Our immediate concern is to solve the problems which we encounter. When we can solve them we find nothing but pleasure and happiness, but failure to solve them often entails suffering and sorrow. Although we try to remedy our wretchedness by our own striving or with other's help, we still find something which cannot be cured by our human efforts. At these times we call for religion as a means of relief and salvation. However, religion should not be sought only in our distress but in our normal way of life.

While we engage in our daily activities, we keep to the force of habit and are prone to be idle if no adequate stimulation is given to us. Here we find our natural weaknesses. This realization is called "the awakening to the reality of life." Usually we consciously or unconsciously avoid looking into the reality of life or we are simply ignorant of the problems which have arisen and developed into our suffering and sorrow. Usually when we acknowledge our failure, we are awakened to the reality of life.

Gautama Buddha is said to be the first man who was completely awakened to the reality of life, so we call him "the Supremely Awakened One." He clearly perceived the non-egoness of our life and the impermanency of this world, and freed himself with diligence from the selfish pursuit of fame and wealth and from the attachment to worldly affairs. We wish to become like him, but even though we try hard to do so we painfully realize that it is almost impossible. Although we persevere stoutly, we find many mistakes and failures in our thought and conduct. Therefore, Buddhism provides for us the clear and sound way upon which we can easily and confidently rely and follow.

Then what should we do according to the teaching of Buddhism? First of all, we should realize that we are a part of a larger Self. Our personal goals are not final ends but are stages on the way to reaching the realm of the larger Self. Here the separation of self from other is meaningless. Instead of feeling jealousy, hatred and greed towards others, what we need is mutual understanding and sympathy. To realize the limitation of our capacity and to transcend it, we must concentrate our minds on the work we engage in, trust others, and be faithful to our own words and deeds. Secondly, we should realize that we are being embraced by the Saving Power of the larger Self. When we encounter misfortune, we must clearly observe its cause, and by all means try to get rid of it. If we find no solution at all, we must realize that it is a momentous occurence since everything is subject to change. We should patiently wait until it passes through and anticipate the Saving Power of the larger Self working in us.

Although nothing can be accomplished on our part, we should never be discouraged. In the course of exercising our beliefs, we will surely find hope and courage and gain pleasure in living. Although these exercises have no ending nor have they an effect on our material wealth, just by doing them diligently we are able to lead our life meaningfully and significantly. Such a teaching can be followed and exercised by all of us in the circumstances we find here and now. Therefore, we call this way of life Buddhism and rely upon it wholeheartedly.

Chapter 2

Buddhism for the Modern World

In 1969, the American astronauts of Apollo 11 success-fully achieved the first landing on the moon. By mak-ing use of highly complicated machinery, they have man-aged to open a new perspective for man's incessant search for more facts about the universe. This attempt is indeed a giant leap to prove the scientific advancement of man-kind. Looking back to the earth on which we live, how-ever, what kind of life are we treading? There are the dangers of constant war, poverty, strife, conflict and tension among ourselves. It seems that there is no pos-sibility of living together in peace. Science has certainly brought us modern contrivances which shorten our labour and give us more leisure in our daily life. How-ever, it does not necessarily solve our life's problems. We are suffering from material, physical or mental burdens, which have shaken the very foundation of our being. Our lives are always threatened by an endless flow of in-security and fear. The man we met yesterday might have an accident and die today. Tomorrow there might be another war which would end our lives. The possession of an automobile or a house is no compensation for inner insecurity and fear. When we come to realize that mate-rial things are necessary but not a primary means to en-

*The front picture shows the image of Bodhisattva Kannon
enshrined at Kofukuji Temple in Nara.*

rich our lives, we seek something spiritual which will satisfy our mind and body.

Unfortunately the present world is governed by materialistic civilizations, and spiritual values have receded backwards to the point of self-destruction. Conscientious people are deeply concerned by this fact, and constantly warn the world of the unsuitability of materialistic rule over man. At this moment the rise of a new spiritual civilization is strongly demanded by people. Of course, there are many forms of religion around us which seem appealing to us, but they only approach us indirectly. Some emphasize obeisance to the religious tradition or custom almost to the point of forgetting other aspects of religious life, and others emphasize routine participation in ceremonies or services, the acceptance of dogma and the authority of the church. Their theological doctrines regarding supernatural powers found in healing or miracles are not easily related to our daily life. Therefore, they become increasingly difficult to understand and practice. Those unsatisfied and yet earnest people, who seek some real solution to the many problems of their troubled lives, some solution that will satisfy both their intellect and sentiment, and do not find it in any of the traditional religions, leave religion entirely, hoping to find the answer in the world of their profession or sensual pleasure. However, they fail to find the meaning in it and become violent, sarcastic or nihilistic about everything that happens, and escape to the world of day-dreaming by doing nothing, taking LSD or marijuana, so that they can no longer face the problems of their lives objectively.

We must be aware that the Sabbath was made for man, not man for the Sabbath. We must be masters, not slaves, of conventional ways of life. In this sense, Buddhism stands out in glowing relief.

1. Buddhism as a Way of Life

Buddhism is not a system of dogmas nor a church building, but a way of life for people who are molded according to Buddhist discipline. Buddhism is pervasive but formless. For that reason, it is difficult to grasp unless we are a part of it and living within it. This way of life was founded by Gautama Buddha about 2500 years ago. He revealed a unique teaching which had not been manifested by any sage in the world. He himself had bitter experiences with life's problems and through his own struggles found the way to overcome them. This way is called the Oneness of Life and has no exact parallel in other religions.

Gautama Buddha perceived that all sentient beings have in common the desire to live and realize themselves in their own way. All cling to existence and are able to survive only at the expense of others. Therefore, he firmly believes that the way we can survive without hurting each other is only by experiencing the basic identity of all life while remaining distinct from it. Our world is nothing but the manifestation of the Oneness of Life where all beings, animate or inanimate, exist interdependently. On this basic ground of life, man imposes distinctions and separates what is "mine" from what is "not mine." This discrimination arises from attachment in man, called blind craving. According to Buddhism, blind craving differentiates Oneness into a plural world of Manyness, and from there arise conflicts, misunderstandings and frictions within man himself. From this blind craving comes the conscious self, affirming its essential selfishness. Because of man's going against Oneness by affirming the blind craving within, he creates an illusory world of Manyness which is not the real world but a world created in his own imagination.

If we understand the importance of the Oneness of Life, we can partake of other's joy, being happy with and for other's happiness, since we are one; and the maltreatment of another is none other than the maltreatment of ourselves. Oneness is therefore the highest truth and the one who realized this highest truth is called the Buddha. The Buddha is accordingly not the God who creates the universe nor a Supreme Deity with a transcendental authority and power. Neither is He a judge who punishes us nor a jealous God who labels man as good or bad. He is rather the guiding light immanent in the Universe. His immeasurable Wisdom and Compassion give us the insight to see the fragility of our human life and the urge to embrace actively all into the Oneness of Life. Thus, we are potential Buddhas; we and the Buddha are interdependent and interrelated. The significance of this Oneness of Life is achieved by realizing the Buddha in man and man in the Buddha. This is not a mystical nor a speculative experience which only qualified men may acquire, but is a spontaneous experience which is manifested in our daily life. Therefore, this way of life can be treaded by any ordinary man, regardless of race, nationality, sex, position, ideology or character.

There is a Japanese saying, "How light the heap of snow would be, if it were piled on my umbrella." When we are aboard a train and something falls on our head from the overhead rack, we sometimes exclaim "Auch!" and endure the pain because it is ours. However, the reaction would be different if it were others'. Even though theoretically we understand that everything falls down due to the law of gravitation we react in different ways; some blame others and some not. Here is a good chance to know what kind of men we are. Whosoever we may be, Capitalist or Communist, Christian or Buddhist, it does not matter. The possession of fame, power or fortune has nothing to do with the problem which we encounter at this moment. Our immediate concern is to solve our problem here and now. When we can solve it in a satisfactory way, we find nothing but pleasure and happiness, but failure to solve it often entails suffering and sorrow.

Once the Buddha was asked by a monk named Malunkyaputta, whether the world was eternal or not eternal, whether the world was finite or not, whether the soul was one thing and the body another, whether a Buddha existed after death or did not exist after death. The Buddha flatly refused to discuss such metaphysics, and instead gave him a parable. "It is as if a man had been wounded by an arrow thickly smeared with poison, and yet he were to say, 'I will not have this arrow pulled out until I know by what man I was wounded,' or 'I will not have this arrow pulled out until I know of what the bow with which I was wounded was made.' " As a practical man he should of course get himself treated by the physician at once, without demanding these unnecessary details which would not help him in the least. This was the attitude of the Buddha toward the metaphysical speculation which do not in any way help one toward genuine religious progress. For them the Buddha says, "Do not go by reasoning, nor by inferring, nor by argument." A true disciple is taught, "Where there is not the Buddha, do not linger on; where there is, pass quickly by!"

2. *Buddhism as an Essential Way of Life*

We are indeed unique beings in the universe and our life is really worth living on the ground that we as *homo sapiens* can understand what we are and what we should be. Our life cannot be substituted nor repeated by someone else, although the transplantation of our physical parts is sometimes possible. Therefore, once we are born in this world, we have to tread our life meaningfully and significantly.

In Buddhism, what is essential for our living is differentiated from the trivials. It is done not through our artificial notion of right-or-wrongness nor good-or-badness, but through our total experience which cannot be transmitted to anyone else. We generally think that words are absolute. We have never been able to break through this condition of understanding; it has been too imposing. But, what is expressed is not the absolute fact.

Words are one of the means which can, orally or through written words, be attached to one's total experience. Thus, total experience is the final text for knowing the essential. Of course, it is sometimes difficult to determine what is essential, but those who tread the Oneness of Life can differentiate it from the trivial. After that, what happens to it depends upon what kind of man is working on it, upon his intelligence, his persistence, and his devotion. It depends upon how clearly and completely an individual can understand a situation and see how he is related to it, and then upon his willingness to translate his perceptions into action. The following is a story which gives us a good example of what is an Essential Way of Life.

In the Edo period of Japan, there lived a Buddhist master called Bankei, who supervised apprentices at his Tensho-ji Temple at Fukagawa, Tokyo. It was the custom in those days that the younger sons of devoted Buddhist families be sent to the temple to be trained as future monks. Bankei once had a very naughty boy among his apprentices who was sent to the temple because of his rudeness. The parents disowned him, expecting that he would be reformed if he entered the temple. However, even after that, he did not correct his behavior. From morning till night, he played around and stole things from the temple, and sold them to the nearby pawn shop. Bad reports spread rapidly, and even reached the ears of the members of the temple. Being unable to remain mere spectators, the rest of the apprentices got together and discussed that the master should dismiss him, otherwise the reputation of the temple, the master, and themselves would be harmed. They demanded the master to take action immediately, and he promised to give them his decision some other time.

A few days passed, and it appeared that no decision had been made. The naughty boy did even worse things. The apprentices were disappointed, and urged the master to make a quick decision. He nodded and asked them to wait for one more day. The next morning came; nothing happened to the boy. This time they got angry and with glaring eyes drew close to the master, requesting, "If you do not have any intention of dismissing the evil-doer, we'll leave the temple, sir." The master received them with a smiling face, and finally spoke to them thus, "If you are so determined, why don't you do that?" Hearing such an unexpected remark, they were astounded and immediately questioned him, saying, "Why do you wish to discharge us instead of dismissing the naughty boy?" The master answered with confidence, "Because you are ready to leave the temple any time, but he cannot do that. If I send him away, he has no place to go." Hearing this, they thought the matter over and felt the deep compassion of their master to the boy. The boy happened to pass by and also heard this, and feeling deeply, he finally reformed himself completely.

This story tells us that Bankei thought that the saving of the naughty boy was the most essential thing to do. He clearly perceived that the boy was able to be educated so he intentionally undertook such a risk. For those like Bankei, the most essential thing is differentiated from the trivial, and is consistently carried out in their life time. They are not surprised at anything that happens on the way; they have nothing to do with the trivialities, either by making excuses or finding fault with others. They always have good poise, because they have deep confidence in the essential thing which is eternally unconditioned and unchangeable. Nowadays, however, it seems to be an inescapable trend that people are easily influenced by environmental factors such as tradition or power of wealth, and are easily contented with the conventional way of life. Because of their lack of confidence in the essential thing, they look around restlessly, and always try to "keep up with the Joneses". These other-directed people can no longer be called unique human beings, because they have become the slaves of a materialistic civilization.

3. Buddhism as an Open Way of Life

"Who knows only his own generation remains always a child." This is the word inscribed in front of the University of Colorado Library. Mature people should always open their hearts to the wider world. However, ego centric people are mostly narrow or closed-minded, and they live only in the dim-cell of their darkened world. They do not progress because they have neither eyes to see things as they really are nor ears to hear something which is better than they possess. They are afraid of simply facing reality directly, and try to protect their confined and dead egos and to cover their inferiority and faults by attacking others. For them, Buddhism teaches the Open Way of Life in order to perceive the Oneness of all life.

It is told in a Buddhist scripture that Sudhana, the way-seeker, went out on a long journey in search of the truth by interviewing people of all kinds because he regarded them as his teachers. He thought the truth was not a particular form of activity, nor had it a particular body, nor did it abide in a particular place, nor was its work of salvation confined to one particular people. On the contrary, he thought it involved in itself infinite activities, infinite bodies, infinite spaces, and universally worked for the salvation of all beings. The truth is immanent in us, and at the same time is transcendent from us: there is no boundary of truth. Our capacities are so limited that we must be humble and modest in bridging the gap between the truth and us. When we think that we are everything and almighty, human tragedy occurs. We cannot become masters or slaves of the universe: we should always be on good terms with it.

Nowadays people do not give others a chance to express their own ideas and opinions, nor do they agree with anyone who promotes new or better projects for the enrichment of us all. These individuals mostly favour or protect certain kinds of people who simply follow or agree with them. When they realize that people are not in accord with them or that there are better things found in others, they get angry and begin to abuse them; or sometimes, out of jealousy, they spread erroneous news or plan secretly to create trouble for them. These egocentric people are mostly seeking their own benefit at the expense or sacrifice of others. They satisfy their own ego by dividing and controlling others. For them, more conflict and strife are bound to come, and there will be no peace among themselves. Prince Regent Shotoku, the great advocate of Buddhism in 6th century Japan, wrote a constitution, in which he said, "Do not become angry just because someone opposes your ideas or opinions. Everyone has a mind and every mind comes to a decision and the decisions will not always be alike. If he is right, you are wrong; if you are right, he is wrong; you are not a genius nor is he an idiot. Both disputants are men of ordinary minds. If both are wise men or both foolish men, their argument is probably an endless circle. For this reason, if your opponent grows angry you should give more heed to yourself lest you too are in error. One can seldom attain all he wishes. Therefore, have a complete understanding of the reality you face and view others with tolerance." If each one of us treads the Open Way of Life, we can certainly bridge the gaps between us and be able to promote virtue in order to become much better people in a much better society in the world.

4. Buddhism as a Together Way of Life

It has been said since the time of Aristotle that we are social beings. From the time we are born until we die, we are always under someone's care, and even for a single day we can not live without having others' aid. Not knowing this fact, there is a strong trend among people to take care of themselves and not worry about other fellow beings. Moral values and a sense of integrity and responsibility have been diluted. People are prone to be diverted, separated and finally alienated from their true selves and from others. They do not know that death is approaching them at every moment. And when they realize that death is inescapable and a concrete reality for them, they begin to fuss and cannot do anything but be stupefied. These helpless people have completely lost the meaning of life, and keep on living in the force of habit until the very moment of their death. For those who do not understand their lonesome and wretched life the meaning of love and compassion toward others is nonsense, because they cannot even love themselves. The Buddha once said, "Man's thought can travel everywhere, but nowhere can he find anyone to love but himself. Likewise, others love themselves more than anyone else. Therefore those who love themselves should extend their compassion towards others."

Buddhism has been regarded as a religion of self emancipation for the monks who have abandoned this secular world. It is also, however, a religion of salvation for all mankind. After the Buddha was enlightened at Budhagaya, he never tired of preaching his teaching to the people around him. If his enlightenment was for his own sake, he would not have preached to anyone else. On the contrary, he preached and the number of his disciples rapidly increased. He sent them into the world with the famous exhortation, "Go ye forth, O Disciples, on your journey, for the profit of the many, for the bliss of the many, out of compassion for the world." His teaching prevailed here and there, and yet was not monopolized by privileged monks; nor was it militantly proselytized or were efforts made to force ideas upon unwilling people. His disciples multiplied, and they formed a fellowship, called Samgha, where no distinction of their background was emphasized. They stood on the same footing and were equally treated in accordance with the ability of each individual. They were instructed to endeavour for their own emancipation, and at the same time to share their experiences with others. Such an inseparable accomplishment found an appropriate expression in the term, Tathagata, which means "one who has gone thus" or "one who has come thus." The former means one who has attained enlightenment, and the latter means one who has come into this world to save others. This notion is attributed to the Budhisattva who is still seeking the truth upward and to share it with others. His life is characterized in a famous parable of the lotus in the mud, told in the Lotus sutra; it emphasizes the point that the merciful Bodhisattva who is born in this world is free from the defilement of the world because of his search for truth, just as the lotus flower is untouched by the mud and water in which it blooms. His vow is that he shall not attain enlightenment until every sentient being is emancipated from suffering and sorrow. It is the nourishing and protecting spirit of a mother for her child; it is the spirit that prompts him to sympathize with the sickness of people, to suffer with their suffering. His purpose in life is always sought in this world to identify himself with others though distinct from them. Togetherness is lacking for the people in the present world who fail to

identify themselves with anything which is really meaningful to them. Here, we must remember that true love
should not be accomplished by looking at each other but
by gazing together.

5. A Buddhist Way of Life

A Buddhist is a person who treads the above mentioned trinity, namely the Essential, Open and Together
Ways of Life in order to achieve the Oneness of all life.
This implies the traditional naming of Three Treasures:
Buddha, Dharma and Samgha, which are the main
objects of devotion for all Buddhists. In the balancing of
these three ways of life is found the legitimate ground for
a healthy and sound life although they are sometimes
interacting and contradicting each other, when they are
sought theoretically.

It is generally said that those who fail to identify themselves with the Three Treasures fall easily into three
categories of personality; namely, epileptic, maniac-
depressive, and schizoid types of men. The epileptic type
of man is mostly adhesive with a strong mind, and
sometimes reaches the point of paranoia. The manic-
depressive type of man is mostly extrovert with an un-
yielding spirit, and sometimes reaches the point of hyste-
ria. The schizoid type of man is mostly introvert and
faint hearted, and sometimes reaches the point of neurosis. These different types of men are, good or bad, intermingled with each other, and form a particular kind of
society or nation in the course of their life history. It
seems that when we go to such extremes as paranoia, hys-

teria, or neurosis, we are prone to become either mad, frenzied, or spiritually dead; there are no alternatives other than these choices. Such an inclination is so deeply rooted in our distorted human nature that in Buddhism we are instructed to always look up the Three Treasures for guidance in order to normalize our onesided character. The Japanese novelist, Soseki Natsume, wrote the novel, "The Three Cornered World" in which he said, "While going up a mountain track, I could not but think the following: When I approach my life rationally, I become harsh. Give free rein to my desires, and I become uncomfortably confined. Pole along in the stream of emotions, and I am swept away by the current. I feel the world of ours to be disagreeable to live in. When the unpleasantness increases, I want to draw myself up to someplace where life is easier. However, when I realize that life will be no more agreeable no matter what heights we may attain, a poem may be given birth to, or a picture drawn."

For those who live in this world, there is no escape no matter how horrible this world is; we have to simply accept it and make a living within it.

Buddhism teaches us more positively that suffering is bliss. Henry Kaiser once said, "I always welcome the bad news, because it makes me stir up." The Japanese novelist, Takiji Kobayashi, said, "Because of darkness, there is light. And those who come out from darkness will really appreciate the existence of light. Our world is not always abundant with happiness. Because of sorrow, there is happiness. Bear in mind that if you want to spend a happy life, you have to taste the bitterness of suffering and sorrow." In our actual life we must painfully realize that encountering problems, desirable or undesirable, is inevitable from the day of our birth, and things do not always go as well as we wish. Often, we have to cope with criticism, hardship, or difficulties when we meet problems. Then, what should we do?

There are three possible ways of solving our problems. The first is direct attack which seems to be the best way to meet them. Most people who succeeded in their undertakings chose this way. This type of man is willing to confront and attack the problem with his own courage and might, and never regret his decisions and actions. A typical example of this type of man is found in the attitude of Musashi Miyamoto, a classical Japanese swordsman. He said, "Under the sword lifted high, there is a hell making me tremble; but attack and attack, and I have the land of bliss." His greatness as a knight is not attributed to his fine skill but to his spirit which made his challengers realize that they were more inferior in skills and motives than he.

However, the majority of us cannot simply, or always follow this way. Therefore, in the second place, a detour is provided for the less strong people. Instead of choosing the way of direct attack, we solve the problem indirectly by adopting a substitute feeling and deed and actively achieve the desired end. William James, an American philosopher, once said, "To feel brave, act as if we were brave, use all of our will to the end, and a courage fit will very likely replace the fit of fear." This detour way certainly helps those who need strength and courage in order to achieve their desired end.

The third method of solving our problems is the way of totally abandoning our efforts. When we are too weak and fail to attack our problems, because of our failure, we are thrown into despair and regret. We are often helpless and blocked in our efforts to solve the problems. In this case, we sometimes react by simply giving up and withdrawing from situations confronting us and escape into the world of day dreaming. We explain our weakness and failure by giving excuses that may be socially acceptable, but there is, in reality, an attempt to hide even from ourselves the true reason for failure. If we have someone whom we can fully trust and rely upon, we can restore our confidence and courage by overcoming feelings of inferiority which may have resulted from failure in the pursuit of solving our problems. Henry Ford once said, "When I cannot handle events, I let them handle themselves." He gives up his hope and effort when he realizes that he has no way of solving the problems. Many people have solved seemingly difficult problems when they gave up their self centered efforts and simply looked upon someone's advice and suggestions. Whosoever he may be, Buddha, God, teachers or friends, the way of self abandonment saves us from the depression of our miserable self.

It is said that there are three kinds of flowers in a pond of lotus, and so in the world there are three kinds of people. Some, rising above the level of the waters or of mankind, have come into blossom; some are already near the light and have only a last effort to make; and some are too deeply sunk in the original mud to come up into daylight. Out of compassion the Buddha preached his teaching of salvation and tried to rescue all of them regardless of their circumstances and capacities. He recommended the way of direct attack for the strong, the way of detour for the less strong, and the way of total abandonment of selfish effort for the weak. It was the Buddha's greatness that he never abandoned rescuing the strong as well as the helpless people, but he extended his helping hands whenever necessity arose.

Buddhism has provided these three ways of solving the problems which are always confronting us. The first way of direct attack can be mainly characterized in the attitude of Zen and Nichiren followers, the second way of compensation found in the attitude of Tendai and Shingon followers, and the third way of self-abandonment is in the attitude of the Pure Land followers. These different types of Buddhism have met the needs of different types of men who seek to solve their own life problems. Whichever we may follow, there is always a common ground on which we stand, namely, the Oneness of Life.

In this way, Buddhism has served its original purpose by introducing many different aspects of its tradition, and people living within it solved their life problems in different ways. Although there exist some discrepancies and misleading elements in the methods adopted to introduce it, Buddhism is not a passive, pessimistic or exotic religion which has in its character feudalistic, magical and mystical elements, but is a part of our heritage brought from the East. It has no connection with the artificial notions of correctness or superiority. It is descriptive and not prescriptive about our life problems. It is practical and peaceful, and is always related to us, our nature, and the dynamics of our development. This I could not possibly find in any other religion. In this sense, I believe that Buddhism will play an important role in the making of more spiritually enriched men if we truly seek the Oneness of all Life in our divided and troubled world.

Chapter 3

Buddhism and Other Religions

Religion is the most important and yet the most neglected thing for people in this contemporary world. Is it not necessary for us any more as a guiding principle for the enrichment of our lives, just like fame, power or wealth? If so, the study and practice of any religion are utter nonsense, and the comparative study of religion is out of the question. Although we can admit that in the past many a bloody strife had occurred in the name of religion, it is an undeniable fact that religion has played an important role in providing the inner security and relief among the people who were molded according to its discipline. Particularly in this divided and troubled world, many people are yearning for the rise of a new spiritual civilization which is trustworthy and applicable to the modern mind. I wonder whether the existing religions will play the same role as in the past to meet the demands of those people. We need to have a unified guiding principle under which each religion has its own place, and where we can find peace and freedom.

There are many religions, institutionalized or not, in the world, and those who believe in them take for granted that their way is eventually bound to win the allegiance of the whole human race. They claim that their way of life is the most desirable and the ultimate one for all to follow, and there seems to be no finality in agreement because of their character of exclusiveness to each other. Here lies tension, conflict, dispute and war. I believe that the truth is one, but modes of its expression are never the same. Therefore, each religion is just like the instrument in an orchestra. The concert cannot go on without the different instruments; no instrument can contribute to the harmony of the whole without regard for the general theme. A noted Japanese Christian Kanzo Uchimura once said, "If all trees would become cherry trees, all birds peacocks, and all people believing the same as I have believed, then I'd wish to get away from this world as soon as possible." An old Buddhist proverb says that there are many paths and roads in forests and valleys, but those who climb up to the hilltop by any of these routes will enjoy the same moonlight on the summit.

Although there are many religions and pseudo-religions in the world, they can be roughly divided into two streams; namely, Semitic and non-Semitic religions. The former is represented by Christianity, Islam, Judaism, and Communism in a sense, and the latter, Buddhism, Hinduism, Confucianism, Taoism and Shinto. I believe that both Christianity and Buddhism are the most talked-about religions in the contemporary world, and are comparatively less attached to any particular ethnic groups or nations, so that in this chapter I would like to take up some basic ideas on the similarities and differences of these two religions, and their peculiarities which would influence the future world. I hope it will not serve as a basis for proof or disproof of superiority or inferiority, but as a tool which we might make use of in our further inquiries into these two religions.

In order to make the study effectively, we must observe three precautions. First of all, we must admit that these two religious phenomena are facts and each is a unique system of thought in its own right. Even though others' views and ideas are hostile or contradictory to ours, we must try to gather and present accurate and undistorted information about them so that we can interpret and compare them impartially. Secondly, we must bear in mind that the comparison of these two religious phenomena must be made on the same footing in the same framework, so that we can avoid partial judgement and disrespect of either of these religions. Thirdly, we must make certain qualifications and clarifications of the terms and concepts found in both religions so that we can avoid the semantic discrepancies and ambiguities of these religious thoughts. Particularly, we must be careful about the translations of Buddhist terms and concepts into English or other Western languages. Such terms as grace, justice, righteousness, prayer, sin, etc. are quite foreign to Buddhism, and yet some Western scholars have misused them as Buddhist terms. With the above mentioned precautions, we can safely proceed to the comparative study of Christianity and Buddhism.

Superficially speaking, there are certain similarities in both religions. They have been founded on the same assumption that there is an ultimate truth, often interpreted as the saving power which transcends the individual. The founders, Jesus Christ and Gautama Buddha, perceived and experienced the ultimate truth and revealed it to their respective followers in their historical and cultural settings. And the teachings they revealed aim at the salvation of all mankind. In order to bring us greater relief they require us to have individual or collective faith and to do certain religious practices. Therefore, from the beginning their teachings have been evangelic, desiring that the rest of the people could be embraced in their teachings. However, these similarities do not necessarily mean identities. There are certain differences in the content of these similar frameworks, namely in perceiving and experiencing the ultimate truth by the founders of these religions. They must be carefully examined in terms of their doctrinal implications.

First of all, the most basic difference between Christianity and Buddhism lies in their concepts of God and Buddha. In Christianity, God is the creator of the Universe in which the world and human beings exist. He is the judge since He is responsible for what He has created in this Universe. He is the Almighty and has the power and authority to intervene the Universal Law of cause and effect. He is the Holy Other so that we can never become God. On the other hand, Buddha is not a god who has supernatural powers but a human being who was enlightened to perceive the ultimate truth. In Buddhism, the known and unknown universe has existed from time immemorial, and though it is in constant flux, nothing can be added or detracted from it due to the law of cause and effect. Buddha is embodied and identified with all sentient beings, and is also subject to that law. He is immanent in us though being distinct from us. Therefore, in Buddhism a personalistic concept of God is quite foreign. The traditional Western reaction has been to label Buddhism as "atheistic." However, Buddhists have their own basic presuppositions in their encounter with the transcendent.

Secondly, in conjunction with the above, there are different views of man in each religion. In Christianity, God created man in His own image by breathing into him an entity called the soul. Because of this soul, man is called superior to the rest of the world. God gives man the right to rule it and use it, since it was made by God to serve man's needs. On the other hand, Buddhism does not talk about man as a distinct entity with an individual immortal soul existing against the rest of nature. Buddhism considers the universe in a unitary way. It does not speak of God and the world, but only of Buddha-nature which is immanent in man and in this mutually inter-relating and inter-penetrating world itself. Therefore, all life is considered most precious and sacred for each speck of life, no matter how insignificant it may seem, has its meaning in the overall universe.

Thirdly, there are differences in the view of man's life problem. In Christianity, the existence of misery and pain is due to man's disobedience or transgression of God's will. Sin originated in the days of Adam and Eve and was a punishment for man's disobedience to God's commandments. Jesus was crucified and redeemed for man's sins, and his whole life was a revelation of God's wish for man's salvation. With this destiny sin-ridden man is helpless unless he repents his sins and is saved by the love and grace of God through faith in Him. So Jesus said, "The time is fulfilled, and the kingdom of God is at hand; repent, and believe in the gospel." His gospel is directed toward the sinners, and not the righteous, and those who have no faith in Him will be punished at the final judgement. On the other hand, the concept of original sin is quite foreign to Buddhism. What Gautama revealed is the Oneness of Life, the experience of the basic identity of all life though having distinctions within it. Because of man going against Oneness by affirming the egoistic Manyness, he suffers. Gautama only taught through his own struggles of life problems, the existence of suffering and the way to overcome it. Suffering is, therefore, a product of man's individual or collective ignorance of the ultimate truth. It is of man's own making due to his imperfections as found in the individual, social, moral and spiritual levels of his existence. Gautama said, "Awake to the reality of life, and know what you are in the context of your surroundings." His gospel is directed toward all who suffer regardless of whether they are sinners or righteous.

Based on these doctrinal assumptions, Christianity and Buddhism have created and developed their symbols, philosophical systems, rituals and disciplines, and have appealed to those who are sinful and suffering. Western scholars in their treatment of religion are primarily concerned with doctrinal problems. But the actual religious life does not consist of doctrines but of other practical elements in every day life. Therefore, we must make clear distinctions between the doctrinal teachings of religions and the experiential content found in the consciousness and behavior of their followers. I have attempted this comparative study of religions in the first sense, and leave the other to the readers, because to study a religion means to experience it, the implication being that there is no other way to study it.

When we glance at the phenomenal side of these two religions, we can not ignore the fact that they are deeply affected by the natural climate and the temperament of those who support them. Some scholars presuppose that Christianity was originated in the vast expanse of cattle-breeding waste land, whereas Buddhism was originated in a fertile farm land. They have spread into the West and East respectively, and formed different cultural patterns among their followers. Accordingly, the characteristic of Christianity is more likely brutal as symbolized in the crucifixion of Jesus Christ on the cross, and that of Buddhism is tranquil as symbolized in the passing-away of recumbent Buddha. Furthermore, it is generally said that the former emphasizes the complete distinction between God and man, subject and object, love and hate, etc. whereas the latter emphasizes the identity of these two opposite components. Therefore, the attitude of Christians seems to be logical, straight-forward and intolerant, whereas that of Buddhists, paradoxical, flexible and tolerant. Although no clear-cut demarcation can be drawn between them, they are just like both ends of the Middle Way.

Florence Kluckhohn, an American anthropologist, once wrote that value orientations are complex but definitely patterned (rank ordered) principles, resulting from the transactional interplay of three analytically distinguishable elements of the evaluative process—the cognitive, the affective, and the directive elements which give order and direction to the ever-flowing streams of human acts and thoughts as these relate to the solution of "common human problems." She classified the relationship between man and nature into three types, namely, Subjugation-to-Nature, Harmony-with-Nature, and Mastery-over-Nature. It seems that the first can be applied to primitive peoples, the second to the Buddhists, and the third to the Christians. This classification cannot be taken for granted as the gradational development of culture from the first stage to the third, but is valid in so far as each man and his society are isolated from, or stand against others. Nowadays the people in different societies or nations are gradually intermingling with each other, and can hardly expand their possibilities without hurting others. Hereby, the mastery of man over or against others is almost impossible: the various ways of thinking and behavior patterns of people must find their places in the context of universal co-existence. At this time, the doctrinal assumption in regard to the differences, if not peculiarities, between religions is less significant than the adaptation of their teachings to our pertinent problems. World-wide secularization is the modern trend, and is in a sense favorable as an attempt to make us known the *raison d'etre* of true religion. However, if such adaptation means the complete surrender of religion to secularism, it leaves nothing but the destruction of all religiousness which is found in the consciousness and behavior of each religious follower.

Now is not the time to look at each other and discuss matters concerning the inferiorities and superiorities of religions, but to look upon something together which will give us the solution to save our divided and troubled world. Coincidentally speaking, the general theme of the Expo '70, which was held in Osaka, Japan, was "Progress and Harmony for mankind" which seems to be characteristic of Christianity and Buddhism. The synthesis of these seemingly contradictory concepts must be the guiding principle for a new spiritual civilization which we may anticipate in the near future. Until the time comes when the world becomes united, I believe that both religions will play an integral part, as told by British historian Arnold Toynbee, and that world citizens will become Christians when they believe in the *progress* of human life, and Buddhists when they appreciate the *harmony* of all life!

Chapter 4

Is Buddhism Atheism?

It has been generally regarded that Buddhism is a kind of atheism since it has no conception of God. Gautama Buddha denied the existence of God or any notion of God which is attributed to supernatural power. According to the definition in the Encyclopedia of Religion (Edited by Vergilius Ferm), *"theism"* is a philosophical term and connotes something more than mere contrast with polytheism. Its essential idea is that of a unitary, personal Being as the creative source or ground of the physical world, man and value, at once transcendent to nature and immanent in it. Theism is thus contrasted with deism, which implies the total transcendence of God to nature, and with pantheism, which by identifying God with nature becomes a doctrine of exclusive immanence. Atheism is, on the contrary, the denial that there is any god, no matter in what sense "god" is defined or the denial that there exists a being corresponding to some particular definition of god. Frequently but unfortunately, atheism is used to denote the denial of God as personal, and more particularly, of a personal God as defined in a particular creed.

Since the beginning of human history, theologians, philosophers, scientists, and even ordinary people have

questioned the existence of God, and expressed their own
idea about God. They defined the nature of God as (1)
the Absolute Sovereign, (2) the "Alone", (3) the Creator,
(4) the first cause, (5) the divine being, (6) the Omnis-
cient, (7) the Ominipotent, (8) Transcendence, (9)
Spirit, (10) Entity, (11) the Redeemer, (12) Immanent
in the world, (13) Impersonal essence, (14) moral value,
(15) Righteousness, (16) Ultimate Reality, (17) Being
itself, and so on. There is no agreement on the definition
and expression of God among them. However, those
definitions can be classified more precisely into two, God
and Godhead. God is the God of the Trinity, the Creator,
and a personal being who can be described as good,
powerful, loving, wise, and the like, and Godhead is the
ground of all being, an infinite essence which can be
qualified only as "Formlessness." Buddhism does not
admit any god in the first sense, so it is called atheism.
However, Buddhism admits the efficacy of Godhead as
the ground of being, so it is not an atheism in a strict
sense. More accurately speaking, Buddhists do not believe in the existence of a God who is defined and accepted by the Christians as a personal being and as a
supernatural power.

It must be remembered that these arguments are only
possible as a philosophical proposition, not as a religious
one. As a philosophical proposition, there are four possible answers to the question of the existence of God: (1)
God exists, (2) God does not exist, (3) the idea of God is
nonsense, and (4) it is impossible to ascertain whether
God exists or not.

First, *God exists*. There are many ways to prove this statement in direct or indirect ways. Decartes once said that the idea of God is an "idea Innata," that is, it is inherent in all men. History shows that many have been keeping in mind the idea of God. Therefore, God exists and has existed for man. The reason is that there could be no definition without the definition of it, namely, there is no smoke without fire.

Second, *God does not exist*. The denial seems to arise mainly from the fact that God is inconceivable and unknowable and accordingly the idea of God seems to be merely an illusion.

Third, *the idea of God is nonsense, and the question does not need to be investigated*. If man knows it is nonsense, he is simply negating the discussion of the existence of God from the beginning.

And fourth, *it is impossible to ascertain whether God exists or not*. This is the skeptic's attitude toward everything. The skeptic tries to avoid any definite answer simply because he does not know what he has experienced.

As a philosophical proposition, we can say that in Buddhism there is a notion of Godhead and therefore it takes the position of No. 1, but as a religious proposition, we cannot say whether there is a Godhead or not. The existence of God or Godhead cannot be proved in a conceptual analysis. It is one's pure experience that grasps the depth of "being" and that becomes "being" itself when one becomes aware of it. So, if we dare to say which standpoint Buddhists would take in the philosophical and religious propositions combined, we would rather answer that "God exists and at the same time does not exist."

We generally think that words are absolute. We have never been able to break through this condition of understanding; it has been too imposing. But, as the *Tao-te-ching* says, "What is expressed is not the absolute fact." Religious expression starts with the fact that the word is only a symbol. It is one of the means which can, orally or through written words, be attached to one's whole experience. If religious experience is beyond logical reasoning, it is not contradicting to say, "God exists and at the same time does not exist." It is even possible to say, "God exists when we say 'God doesn't exist,' " and "God doesn't exist when we say, 'God exists.' "

Although it is possible to argue about the existence of a god as a philosophical proposition, it is impossible to ascertain its existence as a religious proposition. Religious experience is a purely subjective matter; the awareness of God cannot be demonstrated and transmitted to anyone else since it is a total experience. Meister Eckhart says, "Why dost thou prate of God? Whatever thou sayest of Him is untrue." Thomas Aquinas also said that everything he had written up to that time when he actually experienced God was a mere straw compared with the immediate knowledge which had been vouchsafed to him. Likewise, in Buddhism, direct and personal experience is the final text for knowing God or Buddha. There is no other way to prove his existence.

PART II

BUDDHISM IN HISTORY

Chapter 1

Gautama Buddha: the Founder of Buddhism

In many countries and at various times there have been men who, dissatisfied with the conditions of their society or disappointed in their expectations, fled the bustle and deceptive pleasures and wickedness of the world in order to seek in solitude or in sympathetic company quietude and peace of mind. Societies such as the Pythagorean and Orphic brotherhoods in Greece were among those who kept moral precepts and practical asceticism, but nowhere are conditions so favorable for the development of individual religious life as in India. The climate, institutions, the contemplative bent of the national mind, all tended to facilitate the growth of a persuasion that the highest aims of human life and real felicity cannot be obtained but by seclusion from the busy world, by undisturbed pious exercises and by a certain amount of mortification. It was not necessary to form a group or a community to struggle for existence since nature had abundantly provided the inhabitants with natural resources, and little effort was required for those raising crops in the warm climate throughout the year. This accordingly led to an introspective life as each sought his own happiness and understanding of life.

For the Greeks who visited there, this highly indivisualistic life must have seemed strange. Strabon, a Greek geographist, who spent his life in India in the Christian era, reported thus: "They always take their meals alone; no lunch time is definitely fixed. They take meals as they wish. For the Polistic life, the opposite would be much better." The only tie that bound such self-centered individuals was the caste system, in which people were by birth classified into four classes, namely, Brahmin, Kshatriya, Vaisya, and Sudra. No one could escape from this bond if he was born on the soil of India. Besides this, the social conditions of the Buddha's days were unstable: the small countries of Maghada, Kosala and others in Central India were in vie with each other. The evidence shows that in those days there was a great deal of loose living. The power of Brahmins was gradually declining, and the Kshatriya warrior class was dominant. Wondering ascetics vied for the ears of those who sought reality, and hermits were to be found in caves who taught their own spiritual experience. Animism, polytheism, daulism, and even advanced monism; all competed for authority, and within the mess of this society could be found no new hope for those who sincerely wished for spiritual salvation.

It was in these circumstances that historical Buddha was born in 560 B.C. as the son of King Suddhodana and Queen Maya. His real name was Gautama Siddhartha. His father was a ruler of Sakya clan in northern Magadha which was constantly threatened by the surrounding kingdoms. Therefore, his father was anxious to have a son who would succeed to his throne. One day, the

astrologer predicted that the baby to be born would
either become the future ruler or the Buddha. Queen
Maya gave birth to her child at Lumbini Garden on her
way to her parents' home. Legend tells us that when he
was born he took seven steps and pointed to heaven
with his right hand and to the earth with his left hand,
and proclaimed, "Here I am who is destined to be the
most honorable one on this earth." Since his mother
passed away seven days after his birth, he was brought up
by his step mother who spared no pains in the training of
this future ruler. However, as he grew older, his keen
sensitivity made him ponder over the sophisticated court
life, and his uneasiness never ceased but rather intensified
even though he was married to the beautiful Yasodhara
when he was nineteen. When a son was born to him, he
sighed and named his son Rahula the fetter. Legend also
tells us that one day he stole out from the walled palace,
and saw for the first time an old man, an ill man and a
dead man. This horrible sight made him appreciate his
deep sense of impermanence. In order to seek the truth,
at the age of twenty-nine he decided to renounce the
world, and left the palace one dark night leaving behind
him all his worldly fame and luxury. He wondered
around as mendicant practicing samadhi and asceticism
for six years. However he could only gain an exhausted
mind and an emancipated body. Thereafter he gave up his
austere practices, and went to Gaya where he sat under
a pipphala tree and vowed not to rise from deep contemplation till he attained enlightenment. Legend tells us
that while he was in deep contemplation he was tempted

by Mara, but unfettered he finally attained enlightenment
and became a Buddha, the Awakened One, at the age of
thirty-five.

Gautama Buddha remained at Gaya for seven days
and then started for the Grove of Deer Park at Saranath
where he met a goup of five ascetics and delivered them
the first sermon. The Buddha's disciples were multiplied
in number, and their communities were formed as
Samgha. Many monasteries were built at the cities such
as Sravasti, Kausambi, Nalanda and Vaisali with the
help of wealthy merchants and landlords. He sent his disciples to various parts of India and preached to the people according to their abilities and without making any
distinction of caste or class. As water drawn into the
parched earth so his teaching attracted the distressed
people who were yearning for peace of mind. He left his
footprints over almost all of the Central Ganges area of
India.

At the close of forty-five years of missionary activity,
Gautama Buddha went to Kusinagara where he felt the
pangs of illness. He felt his death was approaching but
his mind was calm because he knew that he had done
what he had set out to do. He also knew that his teaching
was universally valid and did not depend on the lives of
its leaders. At his deathbed, he gave his final exhortations
to Ananda and other disciples who had surrounded him:
"Therefore, O Ananda, be ye lamps unto yourselves. Be
ye a refuge unto yourselves. Hold fast to the truth as a
lamp. Hold fast as a refuge to the Truth. Look not for a
refuge to anyone besides yourselves. Decay is inherent in

all component things. Work out, therefore, your salvation with diligence!" Leaving these last words behind him, Gautama Buddha peacefully passed away at the age of eighty.

Chapter 2

A Short History of Early Buddhism in India

What Gautama Buddha taught to his disciples was the deliverance of oneself from the bondage of this illusioned world and the attainment of enlightenment which always entails death to the profane condition followed by a new birth. His teaching was therefore addressed to all suffering people regardless of whether they were ascetics or householders. However, he seemed to assert that rapid progress was to be gained in spiritual life which was only compatible with a retired life. He once said, "Now I tell you of the life which a householder should lead, of the manner in which a disciple should conduct himself. Such duties as are peculiar to the mendicants cannot be fulfilled by one who has a family." Many disciples were reported to abandon their past life and joined the Buddha's community which was known as Samgha. They thought that spiritual life could not be fulfilled in any existing form of society, and therefore formed a confraternity where they were relieved of care for food and lodging and could concentrate on their spiritual life. It should be noted, however, that there was a peculiarity of Buddhist Samgha distinguishing it from other religious orders, that is, everyone was accepted into its community regardless of whatever their ranks in their previous caste might have been. Since they were equally treated, they abandoned their family name and became a "son of the Buddha". In due course, such Buddhist Samgha were expanded as there were many more converts coming into the community, and they set up their own regulations, called Vinaya, in order to maintain it and propagate the Buddha's teaching more widely than ever. Although the Buddha held the life of a mendicant to be necessary for rapid progress toward deliverance from suffering, he highly honored the laity and received the same attention as the monks. After the passing away of the Buddha, however, there were some objections among the disciples to giving the same position to the laity. The Theravadin disciples wanted to possess the priviledges of attaining the Truth by themselves, but the disciples who belonged to the Northern school of Uttarapathaka admitted the laity to the same priviledges. In later years, this controversy gave rise to the development of Mahayana Buddhism in China and Japan in contrast to the traditional Theravada Buddhism which is prevalent in the South East Asian countries such as Sri Lanka, Burma, Thailand, Laos, and Cambodia.

Whichever the case may be, it was the Buddha's Samgha rather than his teaching which first insured for his religion its great vitality and its rapid spread, and which afterwards became a stronghold against the deep-rooted caste system of India. It naturally excited the hostility of the Brahmins and consequently was driven out from Indian soil.

Chapter 3

A Short History of Buddhism
in China

Buddhism was first introduced to China in 61 A.D. when the Han dynasty was powerless to control the subject and was exposed to external threats. In those days Confucian ideology and structure were collapsing and Taoism prevailed among the people. The Han government permitted the spread of Buddhism in order to comfort the people who had a seemingly homogeneous thought in Taoism. They were attracted by Buddhist novel formulas for the attainment of supernatural powers, immortality or salvation. Buddhist scriptures and ornaments were brought to China by the Indian monks who had travelled all the way through Central Asia.

With the downfall of the Han dynasty in 220 A.D., China was divided into two, one in the South and the other in the North. Northern China was governed by non-Chinese rulers who were free from the pressures of traditional Confucian ideology and encouraged their subjects to promote Buddhist practices. Southern China was governed by Chinese rulers but they also were dissatisfied with traditional Confucian ideology, so they began to take an interest in the Buddhist thought. Buddhism not only permeated to the common people but also to the government officials, and the rising popularity of the Buddhist community of monks soon gave rise to the problem between the community and the head of the state. In India, the Buddhist community were refrained from worldly affairs, while in China the emperor was considered to be supreme and everyone should be prostrated before him. When the Northern Wei absorbed all the kingdoms in north China, the emperor Wu-ti felt that the rising Buddhist community of monks had threatened the politics and economy of the state, so he carried out, in 446, the persecution of Buddhism, ordering all the temples, stupas, scriptures and paintings to be destroyed and all the monks to be executed. However, when he died, his orders were cancelled and Buddhism was ever more revived among the people. It was in the Sui dynasty that the emperor finally united north and south China in 589 and decided to utilize Buddhism as an ideology to knit the Chinese and non-Chinese of the entire country closer together. The government assisted in every way possible the building of temples, stupas, statues and in translating almost all the Buddhist scriptures from Sanskrit into Chinese.

When the T'ang dynasty was in power in the seventh and eighth centuries, Buddhism flourished along with the government embracing the whole of China and portions of Central Asia. The Buddhist community of monks also gained materialistic wealth through the acquisition of lands. Contributions of money and foods sometimes far exceeded the needs of the monastic community living in the temples, so were used for the furtherance of the religion and commercial transactions. This prosperity was however interrupted by the persecution of the T'ang emperor in 845. Ever since, the separation of the Buddhist community and the state has been enforced, and the former has independently persued its aim of universal salvation without the patronage of the succeeding governments. The Indian type of Buddhism gradually transformed itself to the Chinese environment and became more Chinese than Indian and finally became a Chinese religion. In the course of time, the new Buddhist schools of thought such as T'ien-t'ai (Tendai), Ch'an (Zen) and Pure Land were established in order to fulfill the religious aspirations of the Chinese, and the Buddhist community in China became more closely identified with the interests of the people. It finally neglected the anti-social and anti-family element of Indian Buddhism and rather emphasized the worldly unity of all life and the universality of salvation.

Chapter 4

A Short History of Buddhism in Japan

1. INTRODUCTION OF BUDDHISM INTO JAPAN

B uddhism was first made known to the Japanese in 552 A.D. when a Korean king presented brilliant Buddhist images, scripture-scrolls, and ornaments to the Japanese Emperor. In those days, Japan was ruled by the Emperor Kimmei and his court nobles. He immediately consulted the court for a decision as to whether or not Japan should accept the foreign cult of Buddhism. The orthodox Mononobe and Nakatomi families strongly opposed this on the ground that Japan already had the traditional religion of Shinto. On the other hand, the Soga family favored Buddhism since they thought it had something to offer for the enrichment of Japanese culture. Endless disputes took place, and the Emperor finally deferred the matter to the Soga family.

လ လ လ

2. THE ESTABLISHMENT OF BUDDHISM AS JAPANESE RELIGION

A bout forty years later when the Prince Regent Shotoku (574–622) succeeded to the throne after the

Emperor Yomei's death, Buddhism was officially recognized as the Japanese religion. He was a great stateman and a devout Buddhist. He felt deeply that only with Buddhist teachings could he make Japan a centrally unified and culturally refined country. In order to carry out his plan, Prince Regent Shotoku issued the Seventeen-Article Constitution in 604 and stressed in it that every subject should faithfully respect the Three Treasures (Buddha, Dharma and Samgha) as the supreme and unmistakable guidance. He ordered the government to build many Buddhist temples among which the most famous one is Horyuji Temple, the world's oldest wooden structure now standing near the then capital of Nara. Besides his official work, he lectured on the Buddhist scriptures known as the *Saddharma Pundarika* (Hokkekyo in Japanese), *Srimala* (Shomangyo), and *Vimalakirti* (Yuimakyo). It was because of his patronage and devotion that Buddhism was firmly established on Japanese soil and became the national religion of the Japanese.

∾ ∾ ∾

3. BUDDHISM IN THE NARA PERIOD
(710–783 A.D.)

After the death of Prince Regent Shotoku, Buddhism continued to flourish among the court nobles, monks and artisans. Buddhist temples, called Kokubunji, were built by the Emperor Shomu in every province, the headquarters of which was at Todaiji Temple in Nara. Buddhist scriptures were introduced from China and without much modification they were studied by the Japanese monks. Buddhist images and ornaments were made by the Japanese artisans, some of which can still be seen in the older temples in Japan. Buddhist temples in those days were the center of culture; they were not only used as places of worship, but also as schools, hospitals, dispensaries, orphanages, and refuges for older people. The monks were also school teachers, physicians, engineers, and developers of many construction projects. Therefore, the Japanese government encouraged and supported the Buddhist institutions and monks spiritually and materially, so that they could work with the government and the people more effectively.

As the numbers of monks increased, they were gradually classified into six Buddhist schools; namely, the Sanron, Hosso, Kegon, Ritsu, Kusha, and Jojitsu. These schools were direct importations from China and were studied at the various government-established temples. The main tenets of these schools can be summarized as follows:

(a) *The Sanron School* was introduced to Japan in 625 by the Korean monk, Ekwan. As its name implies [San meaning three] this school has three canonical texts; namely Nagarjuna's *Madhyamika Shastra* (Churon), *Sata Shastra* (Hyakuron), and the Aryadeva's *Dvadasa-Nikaya-Shastra* (Junimonron). This school teaches that only by negating the belief in existence as well as the non-existence of things can we approach the Middle Way where our spirit identifies itself with the Absolute Reality.

(b) *The Hosso School* was introduced to Japan in 652 by the Chinese monk, Dosho. Although the texts are numerous, the most important one is the *Vijnaptimatrata-Siddhi-Shastra* (Joyuishikiron). This school teaches that nothing exists but our thought. Because our thought creates the world, it is real, and therefore since the latter is a projection of thought it is only a dream.

(c) *The Kegon School* was introduced to Japan in 736 by Ryoben. The main text is the *Avatamsaka Shastra* (Kegonkyo). This school teaches that one speck of life, no matter how insignificant it may seem, is the manifestation of Buddha-nature, and has its meaning in the over-all universe.

(d) *The Ritsu School* was introduced to Japan in 738 by the Chinese monk, Ganjin. The main text is the *Vinaya* (Ritsu) of Tripitaka, the collection of Buddhist scriptures. This school teaches that the strict observance of Buddhist precepts is necessary in order to attain the state of Dhyana and Samadhi, the highest enlightenment. Ganjin established by himself, the *Kaidan* (ordination platform) at Todaiji Temple in Nara where ordinations for all Japanese Buddhist monks took place. Later on, two more Kaidans were established for the convenience of monks residing in the countryside.

(e) *The Kusha School* was introduced to Japan in 658

The front picture shows the image of Infant Buddha enshrined at Kofukuji Temple in Nara.

by Chitsu and Chitatsu. The main text is Vasu-
bandhu's *Abhidharma-Kosa-Shastra* (Abidarma
Kusharon). This school teaches that our "ego"
does not exist. It is merely an illusion. Man is only
the aggregate of diverse elements such as sensation, memory, intelligence, which constitute
reality. These elements are called dharmas which
really exist. Therefore, the ego must be dissolved
into the sea of dharmas although distinct from
them.

(f) *The Jojitsu School* was introduced to Japan in 625
by the Korean monk, Ekwan. The main text is
Harivarman's *Satya-Siddhi-Shastra* (Jojitsuron).
This school teaches that the past and future state
of things are not real, but only the present state is
real. Therefore, each moment cannot be neglected, but should be lived meaningfully.

These six schools were not independent sects, but
existed in one temple side by side just like various depart-
ments in a college, and each school contributed much to
the development of later Buddhist thought in Japan.

∼ ∼ ∼

4. BUDDHISM IN THE HEIAN PERIOD
(794–1185 A.D.)

In 782 the Japanese capital was transferred from Nara
to Kyoto, and accordingly became the Buddhist center of Japan. Soon after, two new Buddhist sects were
introduced from China, namely, Tendai and Shingon.

The six Buddhist schools gradually lost their popularity and were over-shadowed by these two sects.

Saicho (767–822) established himself a Japanese Tendai Sect on Mt. Hiei, near Kyoto, and tried to synthesize all the then existing philosophical concepts. While in China, he studied Esoteric, Zen, and Jodo Buddhism along with the T'ien T'ai Buddhism. He also studied the *Brahmajala Sutra* (Bonmokyo), a modification of Hinayana precepts. Upon his return to Japan he refuted the standpoints of all other schools, particularly of the Sanron and Hosso schools, and instead expounded the Ekayana doctrine based on the Saddharma Pundarika Sutra. It emphasized the belief that all forms of life stood on an equal basis in attaining Buddhahood, so that even conciliation between Buddhism and Shinto was made possible.

In those days all the Buddhist monks had to accept the Hinayana precepts at the Kaidan, otherwise they were not admitted or qualified as Buddhist monks. Saicho, dissatisfied with this rule, wanted to be recognized under the Mahayana precepts which were suitable for Japanese monks. Several times he submitted a petition to the Emperor Saga to open a Japanese Kaidan on Mt. Hiei, and only after his death was the request granted by the Emperor in 822. From this time on, the Tendai Sect gained independence from the older schools in Japan, and from the fetter of the Hinayana precepts.

Kukai (744–835) was a contemporary of Saicho, and he also studied Esoteric Buddhism in China. Upon his return to Japan, he established the Shingon Sect on Mt.

Koya, and expounded the mystical teaching of Oneness with Vairochana Buddha based on the text of the *Mahavairochana Sutra* (Dainichikyo). Unlike Saicho, Kukai did not deny the validity of the Hinayana precepts. He accepted both the Hinayana and the Mahayana precepts and interpreted them according to his own esoteric teaching. He classified Buddhist thought into two parts: esoteric and exoteric, and taught that all sects other than the Shingon Sect were exoteric, because they were known and revealed by the historical Buddha Shakyamuni. On the other hand, in Esoteric Buddhism, truth is hidden and must be revealed. There are in the universe the knower and the known, and they must be identical with Vairochana Buddha through the mystical practices of mantra and mudra in order for the universe to be in harmony. Kukai also classified the then existing concepts into ten parts according to the degree of profundity: 1. No doctrines at all, 2. Confucianism and Taoism, 3. The Sankya and Vaiseshika schools, 4. The Kusha school, 5. The Jojitsu school, 6. The Hosso school, 7. The Sanron school, 8. The Tendai school, 9. The Kengon school, and 10. The Shingon school. According to him, the Shingon sect is the supreme and complete form of religion, while the other schools are lesser and incomplete.

However, the philosophical speculation of Tendai and the mystical ritualism of Shingon had only attracted the minds of court nobles, monks, and scholars who were weary of studying Buddhism theoretically. The mass of the people had nothing to do with these developments of

thought. The monks, belonging to either the Tendai or
Shingon sects, became independent from the six schools,
and defended themselves from the influence of the
government. Once they obtained the privilege of being
monks, they lived together at the leading temples, and
fought each other and sometimes against the government. The institutions lost sight of the original intention
of saving suffering people, and became a third power
standing against the Imperial government and its counterpart. The temple life became lax, and there was
degeneration and corruption among the monks in Buddhist institutions. Seeing this, the ordinary people were
greatly discouraged and deeply impressed by the impermanency and vicissitudes of life.

∽ ∽ ∽

5. BUDDHISM IN THE KAMAKURA PERIOD
(1185–1333 A.D.)

Buddhism was confined to the priviledged classes of
court nobles, monks, scholars, and artisans who had
enough time to master the complicated philosophy and
rituals of Buddhism. It was in the Kamakura Period that
a drastic change took place in the field of religion; Buddhism became for the first time the religion of the masses.
As the new military government was established by
Yoritomo at Kamakura in 1192, three prominent Buddhist Sects were founded one by one, namely, the Jodo,
Zen, and Nichiren Sects. They had common standpoints; they were established on the foundation of the

Tendai doctrine and yet transcended it in their own respective ways.

Honen (1133–1212) studied the Tendai doctrine thoroughly on Mt. Hiei, and yet he was dissatisfied with a teaching which only taught the definition of salvation and the superiority of the Tendai doctrine as opposed to other schools of thought. However, what he wanted was a way to relieve others from suffering and to gain salvation himself. One day he came across the Genshin's *Ojoyoshu* in which he found a passage by the Chinese monk, Shantao, "Only call the name of Amida Buddha with one's whole heart,—whether walking or standing still, whether sitting or lying, this is the practice which brings salvation without fail, for it is in accordance with the original vow of the Buddha." In this passage he at last found what he was seeking. He did not, however, deny the validity of other elaborate teachings and methods found in other schools. But he was convinced that this simple and straightforward calling of Amida Buddha was the only way for him and for everyone who needed relief in that turbulent and degenerate age, because it required no elaborate rituals or complicated philosophy, but only the calling or Namu Amida Butsu which anyone can do wherever and whoever he is.

In 1175 Honen established the independent Jodo Sect which was based on three canonical texts, the *Larger Sukhavativyuha Sutra* (Muryojukyo), the *Smaller Sukhavativyuha Sutra* (Kan Muryojukyo), and the *Amitayurdhyana Sutra* (Amidakyo). He wrote the *Senchakushu* in order to defend his standpoint against the orthodox schools, and preached the teaching of the *Nembutsu* (calling of Namu Amida Butsu) to the mass of the people. However, his ever-increasing popularity among them encountered strong opposition from other schools and the government that in 1207 his teachings were prohibited and he was exiled to the Isle of Shikoku with a handful of disciples. Later he was permitted to return and his teachings were officially recognized. One of Honen's disciples, Shinran, further developed his teachings and established the Jodo Shin Sect.

Shinran (1173–1262) deeply perceived the weak nature of human beings, and had become convinced that salvation could only be found in self-surrender and in complete reliance on the saving power of Amida Buddha. He totally abandoned the precepts of both Hinayana and Mahayana which were "musts" for all monks in those days. Instead he got married and called himself the most wicked man in the world. He simply wanted to identify himself with ordinary men in order to save his wretched self and to pave the way of relief for other suffering people.

Zen Buddhism was introduced to Japan by Eisai, and was firmly established by Dogen. Eisai (1141–1215) studied the Tendai doctrine on Mt. Hiei and then went to China where he found that the Tendai (T'ien T'ai in Chinese) had already declined and the study of Zen was flourishing. He therefore studied Zen and brought back to Japan many Zen texts such as the *Sayings of Rinzai*, the *Hekiganroku*, and the *Kai-an-koku-go*, and established the Rinzai Zen Sect. Zen Buddhism teaches that there is nothing to rely upon but one's true self. Everyone has the Buddha-nature and the potentiality to become a Buddha, and yet it is hidden because of our illusions. The aim of Zen is to throw off one's illusions and all artificial things and to see directly the innermost nature of one's being. In order to awaken oneself and gain the intuitional understanding of life, Rinzai Zen stresses as a means the practice of sitting in meditation and Koan study. The Koan is a sort of pedagogic device which generally is put in the form of a problem. For example, "What was your original face before your mother gave birth to you?" or "When your corpse is cremated and the ashes are scattered to the winds, where are you?" These highly metaphysical questions must be answered immediately without resorting to any kind of logical reasoning process, because Zen is not a philosophical exercise but a way of life. This teaching was greatly favored by the military class, particularly by the Hojo family at Kamakura, and the government assisted the building of monasteries and temples for Eisai and his disciples.

Dogen (1200–1253) also studied Zen in China, and upon his return to Japan he established the Soto Zen Sect. From the beginning, Dogen disliked to engage in worldly affairs and hated to submit to the authority and power of the military government. He built Eiheiji, the mountain monastery, in Fukui, and wrote essays numbering ninty-five in volume. Soto Zen teaches that the practice of sitting in meditation is the sole means to discover our true selves and to attain enlightenment. It does not require any reasoning or inferring. Zen meditation is

not a mystic union with Buddha or the simple confron-
tation of a unique object for one who is putting himself
under a certain prescribed discipline in a particular time
and place, but rather a way of life for everyone in any
circumstances. It teaches a way to live and to die peacefully, meaningfully and pleasantly. This teaching particularly attracted the warriors whose lives were constantly
threatened by their enemies. The *Bushido*, the warrior's
spirit, developed out of its teaching.

Nichiren (1222–1282) studied the then existing Buddhist schools of thought extensively, from which he chose
the *Saddharma Pundarika Sutra* as the most trustworthy
text. He established the Nichiren Sect which is of Japanese origin, and proclaimed that the eternal life of the
historical Buddha is revealed in us. He stressed that by
reciting the name of this text, *Namu Myohorenge Kyo*, with
our whole heart, we can become one with the eternal
Buddha and gain enlightenment. He denounced all other
existing schools strongly on the ground that their teachings refer to salvation only in the next world. According
to him, no texts except the *Saddharma Pundarika Sutra* are
direct and authentic revelation to us who are living in
this world. Since he wrote the *Rissho Ankokuron*, a
treatise in the Establishment of Righteousness in the
Rule of the Country, and tried to persuade the government also to be blessed and ruled by his teaching, he was
punished by the government and exiled to the Izu
Peninsula and the Isle of Sado. Later he was pardoned
to return to Kamakura. He built Kuonji Temple on Mt.
Minobu afterwards and settled there for the rest of his

life. His wordly and patriotic spirit accelerated the rise of the new sub-sects which we see in contemporary Japan.

There were many other fine personalities living during this period but they are somewhat insignificant compared to the above mentioned Honen, Shinran, Eisai, Dogen and Nichiren. No new sects have arisen except a few minor ones during and after the Kamakura Period. These minor sects were more or less the filling-in and working-out of details in the existing sects. That is, after the Kamakura Period, there was nothing that could stimulate the growth of new thought except the flourishing Jodo, Zen and Nichiren sects of the Kamakura Period. Although during this period little productivity in art and literature was seen, a well disciplined and concentrated spirit as well as religious zeal and originality were crystalized by the founders of the newly established sects. Therefore it was a time in Japanese history that almost everything—religious consciousness, active or otherwise—attained its highest peak, and individual minds were freed from all the external bondages which had long obstructed spontaneous growth.

∾ ∾ ∾

6. BUDDHISM IN THE MUROMACHI PERIOD
(1338–1573 A.D.)

Though the military government at Kamakura unified the country and won battles against the two Mongol invasions in 1274 and 1281, it began to decline and collaspse in the next century. Once again Japan was in

chaos and encountered great political and social unrest
with many civil wars. The ordinary people were per-
plexed and could find no place to rest. As a natural con-
sequence, the people were obliged to seek confidence and
reliance in religion. The worship of *Avalokitesvara* (Kannon), the Bodhisattva of Infinite Compassion, flourished
among the people at large.

When the new military government was established by
Ashikaga Takauji in 1392, Japan was once again unified.
More temples and monasteries were built either by the
patronage of the government or by contribution by the
people. Buddhist culture was also highly developed
during this period. The introduction of painting, calligraphy, tea cult, flower arrangement and gardening by
the monks from China greatly influenced the formation
of refinements in Japanese culture that have continued
to develop up to the present time. However, partial favor-
itism of certain sects by the government or the Imperial
Household caused jealousy among Buddhist institutions,
and they either fought against each other or against the
government. Particularly the leading temples on Mt.
Hiei and Mt. Koya became the citadel of the priest-
warriors of the Tendai and Shingon sects. The priests
were more conspicuous as a military and political force
than in their proper sphere. They often threatened the
government and were corrupt in social and religious life.
Zen temples and monasteries, however, became hermit-
ages for the monks who detached themselves from worldly affairs and either concentrated their minds on meditation or engaged in artistic creation. The Jodo and Jodo

Shin sects were rather insignificant during this period, but they quietly and steadily increased their influence among the population.

დ დ დ

7. BUDDHISM IN THE MOMOYAMA PERIOD
(1573–1603 A.D.)

When Nobunaga overthrew the military government of Ashikaga in 1573, he openly suppressed Buddhist institutions because he feared the increased power of the leading temples and monasteries which sided with his enemies. He favored the newly introduced foreign cult of Christianity for purely political reasons. After the death of Nobunaga, Hideyoshi took over his stand and also suppressed Buddhist institutions with the idea of bringing the ecclesiastical completely under the sway of the secular. With the surrender of the Buddhist institutions to the secular power of Nobunaga and Hideyoshi, Buddhist art gradually lapsed into insignificance and was replaced by secular art.

დ დ დ

8. BUDDHISM IN THE TOKUGAWA PERIOD
(1603–1867 A.D.)

When Ieyasu established the Tokugawa government in 1603 at Edo (the present Tokyo), he prohibited the Japanese to leave the country and foreigners to enter. Few exceptions were made. The isolation of Japan lasted for the next 260 odd years; and during that time, Buddhism became purely ecclesiastical. The temples and monasteries destroyed by Nobunaga and Hideyoshi were restored by Ieyasu as comparatively modest and unfortified buildings. Ieyasu personally favored the Jodo sect and assisted in building Zojoji in Tokyo, Chionin in Kyoto, and other temples. He also assisted in building Higashi Honganji for financial and administrative reasons and divided the Jodo Shin sect into two sub-sects—Nishi Honganji and Higashi Honganji. The following successors of Ieyasu also followed his policies and continued to patronize Buddhism and to proscribe Christianity. These measures were taken in order to weaken and control the power of the Buddhist institutions and to protect Japan from foreign invasions. During this period, all temples became registry offices where such activities as births, marriages, deaths, and funerals had to be registered with the priest in charge, and they were accordingly considered family temples. The priests lived in ease and idleness and they often gave the people cheap and worldly instruction.

Despite these unfavorable circumstances, Zen Buddhism continued to show some vitality. Hakuin appeared and re-vitalized the Rinzai Zen Sect with his fine personality and sermons. Basho, who brought into fashion the seventeen-syllable Haiku poems, owed much to Zen. Ingen established the Obaku Zen Sect when he was invited from China to Japan in 1655. Tetsugen published a reprint of the Ming edition of the *Tripitaka* in 1681 which is remarkable for its clear type printing.

However, from the 17th century on the influence of Buddhism gradually declined and was overshadowed by the rise of the rival religious and political philosophies of Confucianism and Shinto. In the first place both Buddhism and Shinto were identified by the decree of 1614, but later due to the roles of Buddhism, Confucianism and Shinto, the three were completely separated; namely, Buddhism functioned in the sphere of religion; Confucianism in the moral; and Shinto in state politics. The idea of separation of these roles was consciously or unconsciously implanted in the minds of the Japanese and is continuously held by them up to the present time. Buddhism was no more a vital religion but retained only its tradition which was handed down by the priests and monks from the Kamakura Period.

∾ ∾ ∾

9. BUDDHISM UNDER IMPERIAL JAPAN
(1868–1945 A.D.)

The Meiji Restoration in 1868 ended the long isolation of Japan and restored the power of the Imperial Household which had been under the shadow of successive military governments for the previous eight hundred years. Japan opened its door to the world and encountered the impact of Western culture and technology. The policy of the Meiji government, therefore, went to both extremes in order to cope with modern nations. Namely, she adopted Western culture and technology as a means of modernizing Japan and re-affirmed the Imperial Household as the supreme sovereignty of Japan. The Emperor was the object of worship as a living god of Shinto; and since Buddhism had no room in this scheme, it was completely separated from Shinto. Buddhist beliefs and worship were banned by the order of the Meiji government in 1868. Many temples and valuable pieces of Buddhist art were either burnt or sold. A large number of priests and monks were forced to return to lay life although this ban was lifted later. The Buddhist institutions were, however, classified under thirteen sects and fifty-six subsects and the founding of any new sect was strictly prohibited.

Fortunately or unfortunately, Buddhism had already been accepted by the Japanese as part of Japanese culture and tradition. Therefore, apart from its religious beliefs and practices, Buddhism permeated even to the lowest strata of the people, and was taken away from few of them. Only a very small number of priests and monks endured and reaffirmed their Buddhist discipline despite the hardships. They also re-evaluated their religion in the light of modern scholarship. However, as time went on, this critical study and application of Buddhism was often interrupted by the nationalistic military government and Buddhist institutions were once again utilized by it during two World Wars.

∾ ∾ ∾

10. BUDDHISM IN CONTEMPORARY JAPAN
(1945–   A.D.)

Since the militaristic Imperial government sur-
rendered to the Allied Powers in 1945, Buddhism
has been neither the monopoly of Buddhist institutions
nor of the government nor of a certain priviledged class
of people. Buddhist studies have been accelerated by the
priests, ministers, and scholars in temples, institutions,
and universities. Ancient treasures of Buddhist art have
been preserved at temples and museums under the protection of the government. Once ruined temples have
been restored and have become centers of study and
worship. International Buddhist conferences have been
held in Japan in which a number of exchange programs
of individuals and knowledge have been initiated.

Now the Japanese have an opportunity to open their
eyes to see Buddhism not only as a part of their culture
and tradition, but also as a religion and a way of life.
Moreover, freedom of belief is assured them. Individual minds are once again freed from all external bondage
and fetters. At this time, they are free to choose their
own belief from the already-established or not-yet established systems of thought, religion, philosophy, and
morals. It seems that they are now struggling to find the
best and most suitable discipline to be the guiding light
of their lives. No one can tell exactly where they are going, but one thing is clear, that is, they will never tread
the same way as in the past. Instead of becoming tools of

an already established culture and tradition, they are becoming fine designers of their own future.

Chapter 5

A Short History of Buddhism in Asia

Buddhism has been, from the beginning of its history, a missionary religion. After the Buddha was enlightened at Budhagaya at the age of 35, he never tired of preaching his experience to the people. The first sermon after the enlightenment was given at the Deer Park of Saranath near Benares where he set in motion the Wheel of Truth. He preached to the people the Middle Way of avoiding the two extremes of sensuality and mortification, the Four Noble Truths of suffering and the way of its elimination, and the Eightfold Path which leads to a happy human life.

As the number of his disciples rapidly increased, the Buddha sent them into the world with the famous exhortation, "Go ye forth, O Bhikkhus, on your journey, for the profit of the many, for the bliss of the many, out of compassion for the world." Thereafter, his disciples started to spread his glorious teaching by setting examples of lives of holiness, perfect and pure for the benefit of all mankind. It was hard work, but his disciples worked as if they were runners with burning torches, pointing out the way to those who were lost in darkness. However, the Buddha's teaching was not monopolized by priviledged monks as Hinduism was monopolized by the

Brahmins; nor was it militantly proselytized or efforts made to force ideas upon unwilling people. Buddhism was readily accepted due to the fact that it simply pointed out the nature, the mechanism and metabolism of the manifested universe, and the way leading from the world of appearance to ultimate Reality.

King Asoka did much for the propagation of Buddhism in the world. Enthroned in 270 B.C., he was at first a cruel king. After killing thousands of people in battle, he felt the horror of war, and was converted to the teaching of Buddha. Thereafter, as head of a Buddhist state, he changed Buddhism from a teaching popular in northern India to a world religion. He sent out Buddhist ambassadors and missionaries to various parts of Asia and the Middle East.

ᛦ ᛦ ᛦ

BUDDHISM IN INDIA

Despite King Asoka's untiring efforts to spread the teaching, Buddhist influence in the Buddha's native country declined around the 7th century. Because of the invasion by Moslems and the corruption of the Buddhist monasteries, Buddhism gradually mixed with the folk religion of Brahmanism, and no activities were seen until the end of the 19th century. There appeared at that time a devout Buddhist named Anagarika Dhammapala who felt keenly the necessity of restoring Buddhism in India. He himself established the Maha Bodhi Society in Calcutta, and maintained the Buddhist holy places in

India. Nowadays the revival of Buddhism is seen among intellectuals and also the untouchables, the lowest caste in India. A few years ago the Indian government sponsored the 2500th anniversary of Buddha's birth at Sanchi and many Buddhist monks and scholars were invited from all over the world.

ᑲ ᑲ ᑲ

BUDDHISM IN CEYLON (SRI LANKA)

The earliest Buddhist missionaries led by Thera Mahendra arrived at Sri lanka in King Asoka's era; and, according to Dr. Le May, "from that time up to the sixteenth century Srilanka was regarded by other Buddhist countries, Siam, Burma and Combodia, with almost as much veneration as the holy places of Buddhism in India, as the fountainhead of pure Theravada doctrines." At present, a majority of the Sinhalese population, numbering 6,000,000, belongs to Buddhism. The project of the publication of the World Buddhist Encyclopedia was undertaken by the Sinhalese government, and to be distributed in 1964 and thereafter.

ᑲ ᑲ ᑲ

BUDDHISM IN BURMA

It is believed that King Asoka of India sent Buddhist missionaries to Burma, the Golden Land. Since Buddhism is the dominant religion, golden pagodas which are symbols of worship for the Burmese Buddhists are seen everywhere, and Buddhist monasteries nearby are the centers of both religious and secular education. About 90 per cent of the people adhere to Buddhism, and the government declared on August 18, 1961 that Buddhism was the state religion.

∾ ∾ ∾

BUDDHISM IN SIAM (THAILAND)

It is hardly known when and where Buddhism was introduced into this ancient monarchical country, but in the 14th century Buddhism almost became the state religion as a king was converted into the Buddhist order by a Theravada monk. Thereafter, the close connection between the royal family and the Buddhist order became a distinct feature of Siamese Buddhism. Sri Lanka, Burma, and Siam proudly maintain their common heritage of preserving at least the original form of Buddhism at it was claimed to be founded by the Buddha himself.

∾ ∾ ∾

BUDDHISM IN CHINA

Buddhism was first introduced into China in 61 A.D. by Indian monks at the request of Emperor Ming-ti of the Han Dynasty. Since then Buddhism has played a vital part in the development of the glorious culture of China along with Confucianism and Taoism. A new interpretation of the Buddha's teaching, which was appropriate to the minds of Chinese, began to take shape in the 7th century, and the rise of the Zen and Jodo sects of Mahayana Buddhism were seen in the 8th century. Nowadays, although no religion is patronized by the government and individual faith is protected under the constitution, many people hold Buddhism as their object of faith. After the revolution, a Chinese Buddhist Federation was established in 1953 in Peking in order to organize the various denominations into one fold.

∾ ∾ ∾

BUDDHISM IN CAMBODIA

Up until the 14th century, the religion of Cambodia was a combination of the Hinduism of India and the Mahayana Buddhism of China. Later, Siamese influence became prominent, and at present Theravada Buddhism is flourishing all over the country. In November 1961, the state sponsored a conference of the World Fellowship of Buddhists, with representatives from more than 25 countries, which was held at Phnom-Penh, the capital of Cambodia.

∾ ∾ ∾

BUDDHISM IN VIETNAM

Chinese Zen-type Buddhism flourished in Vietnam between the 10th and 14th centuries as it was practiced in China during that time, but during many subsequent periods, the religion became a blend of Buddhism, Confucianism and Taoism. In most Buddhist temples the

Chinese version of the Tri-pitaka is used. The recent Buddhist movement became a focus of attention when the native Buddhists actively participated in the anti-war movements.

ಎ ಎ ಎ

BUDDHISM IN LAOS

Buddhism was introduced into this mountainous country about the same time as in Cambodia and Vietnam. Buddhism is the state religion and the royal family is the protector.

ಎ ಎ ಎ

BUDDHISM IN PAKISTAN

Although Pakistan is a country of Moslems, there are a number of Buddhist monks who are active in preserving the Buddha's teaching for the Buddhists of East Pakistan.

ಎ ಎ ಎ

BUDDHISM IN NEPAL

Although the Buddha was born in the Lumbini Garden in Nepal, the majority of the people in this country maintain a tradition of Hinduist, Lamaist and Mahayana Buddhist syncretism. Nowadays the Dharmodaya Sabba is trying to separate Buddhism from the other religious traditions.

BUDDHISM IN SIKKIM AND BUTAN

These are small border countries between India and Tibet where Buddhist Lamaism is the major religion.

ဢ ဢ ဢ

BUDDHISM IN TIBET

Until the 7th century, Buddhism was unknown in this isolated country. When Srongtsen Gampo was enthroned as king of Tibet, Buddhism, introduced from China and Nepal in the middle of the 7th century, became a vital force. It is called Lamaism which is Mahayana Buddhism in tantric guise. Some people call it a mixture of the best and worst Buddhism, and of much that lies between. Buddhism was the state religion until the revolution in 1959. The Dalai Lama was replaced by the Panchen Lama who was on the throne as head of the quasi-religious administration. Under him, innumerable Buddhist monasteries and temples were maintained.

ဢ ဢ ဢ

BUDDHISM IN MONGOLIA

Buddhist Lamaism, introduced from Tibet and China, is the leading religion in this country. The headquarters of the Buddhist monasteries, where hundreds of monks reside, is in Ulan Bator, the capital.

ဢ ဢ ဢ

BUDDHISM IN KOREA

Korea received Buddhism from China in 372 A.D. and immediately afterwards transmitted it to Japan. At one time, various Buddhist denominations existed, but now there is only Zen-type Buddhism which maintains an exclusive discipline in the monasteries. After the Korean war in 1948, Korea was divided into North and South, and both countries have their Buddhist Federations under which more than 500 temples are registered.

ৎৎ ৎৎ ৎৎ

BUDDHISM IN FORMOSA

Formosa was ceded by China to Japan in 1895, and afterwards Japanese Buddhist missionaries were engaged in spreading the teaching of Buddhism to the natives as well as to the Chinese and Japanese living there. After the World War II Japan renounced all claims to China, and Buddhist monks of the Republic of China took over the Japanese missionary work. At present, there are about 2 million Buddhists there.

ৎৎ ৎৎ ৎৎ

BUDDHISM IN HONG KONG

Most Buddhists in Hong Kong are immigrants from Mainland China who are engaged in social welfare work as well as in missionary work.

BUDDHISM IN THE PHILIPPINES

Although most of the inhabitants are Roman Catholics, there are about 40,000 Buddhists who are guided by Chinese monks.

∾ ∾ ∾

BUDDHISM IN MALAYSIA

This is a Moslem-dominated country, but the Chinese monks implanted Buddhism on the soil of this peninsula with the aid of Chinese Buddhist immigrants in the last century.

∾ ∾ ∾

BUDDHISM IN PENANG

Buddhist activities in Penang are confined to the Chinese who immigrated from South China in the last century.

∾ ∾ ∾

BUDDHISM IN INDONESIA

Previously, Indonesia was a Buddhist-dominated country as can be seen from the Buddhist remains in Borobudur and Tjandi Menbur. However, after the invasion by the Moslems in the 14th century Buddhism declined rapidly, and only recently has it revived again.

In 1952, the Tri-Liherma Federation in Indonesia was established.

∞ ∞ ∞

BUDDHISM IN AUSTRALIA

A Buddhist nun named Dhammadina came to Australia as the first Buddhist missionary in the beginning of this century. Today, there are a number of Buddhist societies actively carrying on the spread of the Buddha's teaching.

Chapter 6

A Short History of Buddhism in the West

I t is noteworthy that during the last twenty years Buddhism has rapidly become a focal point of interest
with Westerners who had no knowledge of it previously. Except for a few Asians who settled in the West or a
number of specialized scholars, Buddhism had simply
been regarded as one of the exotic religions which was
practised by Asians in remote corners of the world. But
nowadays it has made its appearance on Broadway and
has become the most talked-about non-Christian religion
in the West.

Buddhism in the West has width and depth. From
our ministers to Sunday School children; from university
professors to mental patients; from the reader of *The New
Yorker* or *The Paris Match* to the beatnicks or the hippies;
from museum specimens to ten cent bric-a-brac; and
from snow-ridden Scandinavian countries to Aloha
Hawaii, Buddhism has permeated so thoroughly that it
has become difficult for us to recognize how deep and
wide the influence of Buddhism has been laid upon the
peoples in the West. In this short article I would like
first of all to divide this chapter into two parts; (A)
Buddhism in Continental America, and (B) Buddhism in

Europe, and to discuss the historical development of Buddhism at various countries.

∾ ∾ ∾

1. History of Buddhism in Continental America

BUDDHISM IN HAWAII

The introduction of Buddhism to Hawaii began with the arrival of Rev. Soryu Kagai of Nishi (West) Hongan-ji school of the Jodo-Shin denomination in Japan to Honolulu in 1887. In those days, an innumerable number of Japanese immigrants were employed under limited or free contracts on sugar and pineapple plantations. They worked only with the idea of making a quick fortune, and going home loaded with honors. The hardships of heavy labor and the cruel treatment by their white employers, as well as the low wages and poor facilities were the conditions under which they worked from morning till night. In this period of adversity, Buddhist missionaries arrived and exerted themselves to the utmost only for the welfare of those who desperately needed spiritual guidance. There are tales that a Buddhist minister who carried the statue of Buddha on his back and made his rounds of the plantation camps often encountered strong opposition from camp residents, and yet never gave up his missionary zeal even when he was denounced and expelled by them. However, after a series of tireless visitations, they gradually began to ap

preciate his efforts and he finally obtained a congregation at a small cottage where he put up a wooden plate
engraved, "Here is the tiny shrine of Amida Buddha
which was brought all the way from Japan." Afterwards,
despite their unstable life, many other Buddhist missionaries made shanties their temples where they performed
all kinds of ceremonies and gave terakoya-type Japanese
language instruction and all possible advice and care to
the Japanese immigrants. Fortunately, the nature of
Hawaii is exceedingly benign; a mild climate all the year
round gave them cool showers and gentle breezes
brought at intervals by the trade winds from the Pacific
Ocean. All the fatigue they accumulated through their
incessant labor gave way to encouragement and hope in
their miserable lives.

After the final victory in the Sino-Japanese war in
1895, Japan greatly strengthened her power, and accordingly the treatment of the Japanese immigrants in
Hawaii was gradually alleviated. By this time there were
already 50,000 or so of Japanese immigrants with their
80,000 children born in Hawaii, and therefore they
partly gave up their long cherished hope of going home.
They entered into their own businesses with the nullifica-
tion of their contracts with the plantations. Their living
standards greatly improved and the constant disorderli-
ness of the Japanese community gradually disappeared.

Increasing numbers of Buddhist missionaries had ar-
rived by this time, dispatched by the major Japanese
Buddhist denominations. The headquarters of the Nishi
Honganji and Jodo denominations felt the need for

missionary work in Hawaii, and promptly raised the head-temple in Hawaii to the rank of sub-headquarters (Betsuin). As they were unable to obtain financial aid from their headquarters, the resident ministers in Hawaii were fully determined to support themselves. Despite the disasters of pestilence and big fires which struck Honolulu in the 1900s, they built more temples with the full cooperation of many lay members who were mostly responsible for the financial aid. Following them were the Soto, Shingon, Higashi (East) Honganji and Nichiren missions which started their missionary work by the late 1910s. In order to avoid unnecessary friction among themselves, they set up the Hawaii Buddhist Council for mutual help which has successfully continued up until now. It sponsors the state-wide celebrations of *Hanamatsuri* (Buddha's birthday) and *Jodo-e* (Buddha's enlightenment). It is worthwhile to mention also the establishment of the Young Buddhist Association and the Japanese Language Schools as part of the incidental missionary work of the temple.

As time went on, Buddhist activities in Hawaii grew in prosperity, but on December 7, 1941, they received the greatest blow ever known to them. Immediately after Japan's attack on Pearl Harbor followed by the Declaration of War against the Allied Nations, Japanese Buddhist ministers and their supporters were confined and later transferred to concentration camps on the mainland U.S.A. All the Japanese Buddhist temples and their affiliated schools were taken over by the U.S. government and the doors were closed to their members. For four years during the war time they spent uncertain lives with broken hearts, and Buddhist activities in Hawaii seemed to be at an end. However, because of the constant appeals and petitions made by the remaining members to the U.S. Government, Buddhist temples were fortunately not destroyed.

Like the Israelites who returned from exile in Babylonia, Japan's surrender to the Allied Nations in 1945 made it possible for all the confined Japanese ministers and their supporters to return to Hawaii from the concentration camps. They returned penniless and despaired at the sight of seeing their ruined temples. However, they could not stand by only looking at the members coming back to the temple by twos and threes. They started working from practically nothing: they brought the members together and conducted services commemorating their happy reunion and the memory of the war dead. Diligence and the loyalty of the Japanese Americans to the United States were shown by the members of the All Nisei 100th Infantry Battalion. The 442nd Regimental Combat Team at the Italian battle front was extraordinary and highly praised by its fellow Americans. They quickly dissolved the racial discrimination against the Japanese Americans. Due to the Korean war which followed the war industries and services brought prosperity, and the responsibility with other Americans for having Americans in Hawaii was tremendously improved.

Now the Japanese population far exceeds 200,000, one third of the total population of Hawaii, and the able Japanese Americans are no less better than the Caucasians to play an important role in the business and political world. Right after Hawaii's admittance as the 50th state in 1960, they felt proud of sharing equal rights and the responsibility with other Americans having built up a democratic nation.

Along with the increase of Japanese-Americans, the Buddhist missionary work in Hawaii underwent a drastic change; Buddhist missionaries attempted to turn a misfortune into a blessing by the prompt reconsolidation of their temples after they were re-requisitioned by the U.S. government. The re-opening of the Japanese language schools, the repair work and the reconstruction of new temples were launched by them with the full co-operation of their members. At present, the Buddhist temples of Honpa (Nishi) Honganji, Jodo, Soto, Shingon, Higashi Honganji, Nichiren and other denominations are located on all the islands, the total number of which far exceeds 90. As for resident ministers there are more than 120 who are doing their utmost in their missionary work day and night.

As for the academic study of Buddhism we should not neglect the existence of the University of Hawaii in Honolulu. The East and West Philosophers' Conference is held every four years at the University Manoa Camps where world renowned Buddhist scholars such as Dr. Junjiro Takakusu and Dr. Daisetz Suzuki are invited to give lectures and free discussions. In 1962 the East and West Center was established at the University where the exchange scholars and students from both East and West do their research work intensively. The Inter-faith seminar was initiated by the leading Buddhist and Christian ministers in Honolulu who exchange their views and opinions and sometimes invite guest speakers from different faiths.

Hawaii is indeed the crossroads of the world where things Oriental are imported and harmoniously blended with the Western culture. Under a tropical sky they co-exist and can hardly distinguish their origins. The Japanese Garden at the East and West Center or the Three-storied Buddhist Pagoda in Nuuanu Valley reminds us of the Oriental atmosphere, so that when we are there we feel as if we were in Japan. The Chinese New Year's festivity in downtown Honolulu or the Japanese Bon dances at the various Buddhist temples are colorful and gay, and many native and tourist *haoles* participate in these events with their fellow Orientals.

 భు ఎు ఎు

BUDDHISM IN THE MAINLAND U.S.A.

The history of Buddhism in the mainland U.S.A. began at the end of the last century when the first Japanese Buddhist missionary, Rev. Sokei Sonoda, visited San Francisco in 1899, where he started missionary work among the Japanese immigrants. Since then rapid progress has been made by untiring missionaries and their supporters who have built temples, schools and dormitories. Although the last war naturally caused a serious interrruption in the activities, a new period of temple activity began when the Buddhist missionaries returned to their temples from internment after the war and has continued up to the present.

There are now more than 100 Buddhist ministers of Japanese, Chinese and American descent, who are officiating in their respective temples. The number of temples is little less than the number of ministers. There are more then 100,000 members enlisted at the Buddhist Churches of America, Higashi Honganji Mission, Jodo Mission, Nichiren Mission, Rinzai Zen Mission, Shingon Mission, Soto Zen Mission and other various temples, clubs and associations.

Nowadays, Buddhist activities are not confined to a particular ethnic group, but are open to Americans of all races. A number of Buddhist societies have been established throughout the United States, and their membership is gradually increasing. It has been, however, pointed out with criticism that Buddhist missionaries have converted few non-Buddhist Americans to their religion, and have succeeded in building very few Buddhist museums and libraries in their communities. Besides, those who are attracted to Buddhism are regarded as outcastes of American society. This makes it clear that there are many things to reconsider and renovate in the system and method of missionary work. We must remember in this connection that the first Protestant missionary to the Far East spent seven years on his first convert—his cook!

Buddhist studies in America were initiated by a number of American scholars such as Henry Clarke Warren and Paul Carus right after the World Congress of Religions which took place in Chicago in 1893. Since then an increasing number of scholars have been engaged in research work on Buddhism, although regrettably they are little known to Americans in general.

As for personal influence on Americans, the presence of the late Dr. Daisetz Suzuki, an authority on Zen Buddhism, is great. In 1957 *the New Yorker* ran a fourteen page profile of Dr. Suzuki, and a year earlier Harper's *Bazaar* printed a page-sized portrait photo of him. The latter carried the comment that "an ever increasing number of Westerners are paying tribute to the stunning spiritual insights of this man, who sees beyond the duality of thought and language to the heart of reality itself." He was actually the pioneer of Buddhism in America, having written more than 50 books on Buddhism both in English and Japanese, and he imparted a certain warmth to American audiences at all times wherever he was.

There have been a number of American scholars, psychiatrists, philosophers, novelists and artists under Suzuki's tutelage. For example the renowned psychiatrist, Erich Fromm, recently wrote a book entitled, *The Art of Loving*, which is certainly influenced by Buddhism. Some other scholars like Van Meter Ames and Paul Wienpahl suggest some striking resemblances between Buddhism and contemporary Western philosophy such as pragmatism and existentialism, and still others like Alan Watts show the uniqueness of Buddhism where it transcends any contemporary Western philosophy.

In a recent issue, the *Time* magazine noted: "Zen

Buddhism is growing more chic by the minute." The
Zen boom is still going strong from university professors
to socialites, from psychiatrists to beatnicks. Newly-coin-
ed words have been invented to differentiate the categories of Zen, such as Beat Zen, Cocktail Zen, Square
Zen, Zen beyond Zen and so on. No one knows how long
this boom will continue, but there is the sign that it is
going to enter a period of incubation in order to grow as
the real native Zen in the soil of America.

Turning from the popular aspect of Buddhist studies
to the academic one, we note that there are quite a number of extensive studies on Buddhist history and thought
which are being undertaken by various scholars at major
American institutions. Recently the phenomenological
studies to understand the social and political impact on
Buddhism have become quite popular among the scholars as opposed to the ontological ones. We can hardly
find great scholarship yet in this country, but it is hopeful
that within the next few years a higher level of attainment will be reached if sufficient opportunity and stimulation are given to the rising young American scholars. At
the present time, courses on Buddhist studies are offered
by the following institutions: University of California
(Berkeley and Los Angeles), Stanford University, University of Oregon, University of Washington, University
of Nebraska, University of Wisconsin, University of
Chicago, University of Cincinatti, Oberlin College,
Claremont College, University of Pennsylvania, University of Michigan, Princeton University, Columbia
University, Yale University, University of New York,

Colgate University and Harvard University. Journals such as *Philosophy, East and West, Journal of Religion, Journal of the American Oriental Society, Journal of Asian Studies* and *Harvard Journal of Asiatic Studies* are periodically published, and often contain valuable articles on Buddhism.

In the past few years things Oriental have made their way into Museums, galleries, schools, home, parks, department stores and even the five-and-ten-cent stores. Not only Buddha's statues, images, and pictures, but even such things as miniature temple-bells and incense-burners are on display.

Some of the major displays that have made the circuit of American museums and galleries have consisted of paintings by Tessai, Toko Shinoda and Shiko Munakata whose inspiration is certainly drawn from Buddhism. A great number of books on Asian art and culture have been published in this country. Books on all aspects of Asian culture such as music, drama, *judo, karate,* tea-ceremony and flower-arrangement are in wide circulation. Even an unfortunate contribution of Zen to American Literature is seen in Kerouac's novel, *The Dharma Bums,* a best seller. In this novel the younger generation's non-participation in the American way of life by giving itself up to pointless frenzy, adolescent bombast, and libertine interpretations of personal freedom, is vividly described.

The Buddhist blend of simplicity, directness and profundity is elsewhere so flourishing that we may sometimes wonder what is Buddhist and what is not. Whatever it may be, the digestive power of such aesthetic values found in American audiences is tremendous, though ironically this kind of approach has been institutionalized less than anything else. In any case, Buddhism in art is a major source of joy and attraction, and will no doubt play an important role in introducing Buddhism to the non-Buddhist Americans in this country.

∾ ∾ ∾

BUDDHISM IN CANADA

Buddhism in Canada can be regarded as the offshoot of Buddhism in the United States. In 1888, there was a man called Mr. Nishimura who established the first Buddhist congregation at his home in Westminster near Vancouver. After the establishment of the first Buddhist temple in 1905 at Vancouver by Rev. Senju Sasaki, the number of temples and their membership multiplied, and now there are about 18 Buddhist temples, all belonging to the Honpa Hongwanji school of the Jodo-Shin denomination.

Right after World War II, the Japanese immigrants who had been detained in concentration camps were freed and settled in the East. They needed spiritual guidance from Buddhist ministers who had been dispatched from Japan. However, the first generation Japanese who settled there are gradually being replaced by the second and third generation Japanese who were born in Canada. In the past, missionary work was limited only to the Japanese-speaking immigrants, but now it is widely open, not only to English speaking Japanese Canadians, but to all other races as well. Therefore, in order to meet their demands, the Buddhist Churches of Canada was established in 1968 as an independent organization, and the American-born Bishop Newton Ishiura was chosen as the first leader of this organization.

The academic studies on Buddhism are mostly centered around the major institutions such as the University of British Columbia, the University of Toronto and McGill University where Buddhist scholars are being invited to give their lectures on a temporary basis.

The Buddhist influence on the Canadians in general is insignificant except for those who immigrated from Asia. However, the World Exposition in 1966 in Montreal has certainly given an impetus to the Canadians to know more about the varieties of cultures outside Canada.

∾ ∾ ∾

BUDDHISM IN BRAZIL

Rev. Seijiro Ibaraki of the Butsuryu denomination of Nichiren Buddhism was said to be the first Buddhist missionary. He brought together the Japanese immigrants at his home in 1908, and later he built the temple, called Taisenji at Lins City. Although Brazil is a Catholic dominated country, freedom of belief was assured in the Declaration of Independence in 1889, and varieties of religions came ashore to this continent. Since then, rapid progress of Buddhist missionary work has been made, although it was interrupted by World War

II. A new period of Buddhist activity began right after the war, and has continued to the present. At present, there are about 40 temples of seven Japanese Buddhist denominations, and an almost equal number of ministers presiding in the temple.

So far Buddhism in America has served its original purpose by introducing many different aspects of Buddhist tradition, thought and art to this continent. Buddhism, which was initially intended for Asians, is now facing a new situation brought about by the native peoples who show a keen interest in it. It is no more a foreign religion but a part of American heritage brought from the East. Therefore, it can be shared with others like Christianity and Judaism which were brought from the West. In this sense, we must distinguish "American Buddhism" from "Buddhism in America" though these are closely inter-related. The former must be grasped and expressed by native Americans as a universal religion, which gives them legitimate grounds for their way of life and thought. On the other hand, the latter cannot be an American religion so long as it is considered something alien by fellow Americans. Buddhism on the American continent is now in the process of transforming from its traditional form into the new one, so that it can implant the significant Buddhist faith and teaching on the Americans who can find something meaningful in them. It is understandable that modern life places innumerable obstacles in the way of American Buddhism, but no one should be discouraged. If American Buddhism is definitely necessary to and important for Americans in their achievement of true freedom and peace, there is room for Buddhism and a bright future for its further development in this vast continent.

〜 〜 〜

2. History of Buddhism in Europe

Unlike on the American continent where Buddhism was brought from the East by the Asians, the introduction of Buddhism in Europe was from the beginning, at the initiative of the Europeans themselves. No one knows when and from where Buddhism was introduced to Europe. It is, however, possible that Buddhism was known right after the invasion of Alexander the Great to India in 325 B.C.; his army brought back some information about the customs and traditions of India to Europe. Some scholars find resemblances of Buddhism with Manichaism, Gnosticism and neo-Platonism in the West, and assume it has the same origin as these systems of thought. Some others flatly deny this assumption, saying that the resemblances are coincidental. At any rate, the traffic between the East and West increased and made possible the inflow of Eastern thought and things Oriental into Europe and vice versa. However, this free flow of inter-exchange was abruptly interrupted by the invasion of Islams in the 7th century. The intolerant Islams who took over Southern Europe became the main obstacle to introducing any foreign culture into Europe.

After the withdrawal of the Islams from the 16th century onward, Europe became a predominant world power. Along with the rise of modern science and its application to human life, the Europeans made their appearance in every corner of the world and proselytized the barbarians as they thought of them, with their highly developed culture and might. So far the contact between Europe and other countries was superficial and fragmentary, but in the interest of Europe, they became more persuasive and single-minded than ever before. At this point, Buddhism as one of the most influential religions in the East has become a focal point of interest with them.

From the 16th century onward, the European colonialism continued in the East. The Christian missionaries who were dispatched from Europe settled in India, Ceylon (Srilanka), Siam (Thailand), Cambodia, China and Japan along with the merchants who wished to trade with the East. They brought back things Oriental and introduced the customs and traditions of the East to Europe, and later accelerated the rise of enlightenment philosophy and literature in the 17th and 18th centuries. The reaction of European intellectuals who received Asian religions was divided into two extremes: those who proved the superiority of their own religion and those who found something meaningful in Asian religions. Their attitude toward the East was more subjective and straight-forward so that the East had been regarded in a distorted image by the Europeans.

However, at the turn of the 19th century, the situation of Oriental studies has changed into a new phase. More objective studies were necessitated by a number of European scholars such as Eugene Burnouf, T.W. Rhys

Davids or Hermann Oldenberg, who wrote books on Buddhism based on their linguistic research. Their interests were centered around India rather than China or Japan as they were unable to reach the materials of the Far East in those days. They traced the origin of European languages to Sanskrit which is regarded as the Indian classical language, and made their utmost efforts in translating the important religious texts of India. The establishment of the Pali Text Society in London in 1882 by Rhys Davids, who had translated and published a number of Pali Buddhist texts, is worthy of mention. *The Sacred Books of the East,* edited by Max Muller, have been published since 1879, and number 51 volumes at present. These linguistic works, translating most of the important religious texts of the East, played an important role in accelerating the comparative study of religions among European scholars. Arthur Schopenhauer was one of them who acknowledged the universal truth found in the teaching of Buddhism. More extensive studies on world religions were expected in the 20th century when the scholars travelled and learned much about the religions linguistically, anthropologically, sociologically and politically. Initially their studies on Buddhism were superficial, but at the turn of 20th century there appeared a number of Westerners who called themselves disciples of the Buddha and endeavored to propagate his teachings. They were greatly influenced by the success of Sir Edwin Arnold's book, *"Light of Asia"* which was published in 1879. They were also attracted by the establishment of the Theosophical Society in New

York in 1875, headed by Captain H.S. Olcott and Madam H.P. Blavatsky.

∾ ∾ ∾

BUDDHISM IN ENGLAND

Initiated by the above-mentioned movement in the past centuries, those who claim themselves as Buddhists established the Buddhist Society of England in 1906, headed by R. J. Jackson and J. R. Paine. They soon got in touch with Allan Bennet and J. F. M'Kechnie who were in Burma as Buddhist monks, and together with them the Buddhist Society was expanded into the Buddhist Society of Great Britain and Ireland. When Allan Bennet under the Buddhist name of Ananda Metteya returned home from Burma, the Society headed by Rhys Davids had gradually transformed its activity from academic study into a living religion for western people.

Ever since, the membership of the Society has steadily grown, although its name has been changed a number of times. Presently, the London Buddhist Society headed by Christmas Humphreys since 1924, is the oldest and largest Buddhist organization in Europe, and has a quarterly magazine, "*the Middle Way*" which attracts many Westerners to Buddhism. Besides this society, there are a number of Buddhist organizations in Cambridge, Manchester, Oxford, Edinburgh, Birmingham and Brighton, where the meetings are being held regularly.

∾ ∾ ∾

BUDDHISM IN FRANCE

"*Les Amis du Bouddhisme*" was the first Buddhist organization in France founded by Miss Constant Lounsbery in 1929 in Paris. Although this organization was promoted by the Ven. Tai-Hsu of China, it is largely of Theravada Buddhism. Its organ paper, *La Pensee Bouddhique,* is being published bi-monthly, and has a wide circulation. After the war, Mahayana Buddhism was introduced by the Japanese Buddhists who established a number of Buddhist organizations in France, but its influence can not yet be defined in a concrete form. However, the contribution of French scholars and Catholic fathers who have published a number of books on Buddhism, is remarkable. Their works are sometimes translated into English and are available to the readers.

∾ ∾ ∾

BUDDHISM IN GERMANY

In Germany, Karl Seidensticker established the Buddhistischer Missionsverein in Deutschland in 1903 in Libtische. Ever since, a number of Buddhist societies have been established, such as the Western Vihara headed by Dr. Paul Dahlke at Frohnau or the Buddhistische Haus headed by Georg Grimm. After the war the number of societies has multiplied, and in 1958 they formed the Deutsche Buddhistische Union in order to give each other mutual assistance. The membership has also increased, and some of them have travelled to the East and became Buddhist monks like Nyanatiloka.

The Buddhist influence upon the Germans was evident ever since Arthur Schopenhauer. After him were a number of philosophers, novelists and artists like Edmund von Hartman, Friedrich Nietzche, Herman Hesse, Georg Grimm, Johann W. Goethe, Adolph H. Wagner and so on, upon whom the Buddhist influence was remarkable.

Buddhism was also widely studied and practised in other European countries such as Austria, Holland, Belgium, Hungary, Poland, Finland, Sweden and Switzerland, and numerous societies have come into being. Their membership is increasing, and they send their delegates to the World Buddhist Conferences which are held every four years in various Buddhist countries.

After the war, Buddhist activities have accelerated in various countries in the West. However, they cannot be overexaggerated: their activities are rather confined in their organizations, and hardly come up as an influential power in their society at large. Those who have committed themselves as Buddhists can be regarded as outcasts who were dissatisfied with their traditional European religion and society. They take refuge in the minority group of Buddhists, and are trying to become forerunners of the new world. It is evident that an increasing number of Westerners has been attracted to the unique teaching of Buddhism. They will always be out of all proportion to the number of Buddhists. The question of how and when they can be drawn to Buddhism will hardly be answered unless the elucidation of purpose and method of the Buddhist way of life is sufficiently provided by the Buddhists themselves. There are problems which are confronted by both Buddhists and non-Buddhists. The possibility of introducing Buddhism to Europe is made possible by interplay between provider and receiver. The former must be well acquainted with the psychology of the latter and his social structure, and at the same time he must have something meaningful to offer on his part. The latter should feel the necessity of receiving it and become a part of it.

The good is subordinated to the better, and the better to the best. The better man and thing will win out if the right chance is given to them. In this sense, the most urgent need for us is to provide first-grade religious men of intellect and the most refined things which are far superior to what can possibly be found in the West. I was once told that the contribution of one Dr. Daisetz Suzuki to Western culture far surpasses that of 100 Japanese Dietmen who have visited the West. The actual contribution of Buddhism to the West must, however, be made by both Buddhist missionaries and Western Buddhists. The task for the former is to become transmitters for the heritage of Buddhism, enabling it to be brought to Western Buddhists, and for the latter to adopt and make use of it for their own salvation and for the further introduction of it to future generations of Westerners. Of course, no sharp difference in role can be made between them since religion moves from heart to heart. But we cannot ignore the fact that for an average Westerner his life is deeply affected by his religious and social environment. On one hand, there is a great tradition of Christianity, and on the other modern secularism, naturalism, nationalism and humanism. Greatly influenced by and itself influencing these two camps, Buddhism will tread the Middle Way and play an important role in changing the course of Western culture and a way of life in the near future.

PART III

BUDDHISM IN TRADITION

Chapter 1

The Teaching of the Jodo Mission

So far many people have adopted every possible means in order to gain salvation, but they seem to fail because of the limitations of human capacity. They have found that the harder they try by their own efforts the more they fail. We can well understand this when witnessing the fierceness and dreadfulness of war, floods, and earthquakes, and, not being able to prevent them, we gaze upon them helplessly. When we are thrown into despair because of illness or bankruptcy, we cannot avoid relying upon others for help. This may be a natural result of our sentiment. If a person is in a position to discern his nature as completely and accurately as possible in its naked state and to realize his weakness and the limitation of his capacity, then, his religious sentiment, regardless of the name used, is already beginning to show a definite sign of awakening. A noted Japanese critic, Katsuichiro Kamei, quoted the three occasions for the awakening of religious sentiment. They are, firstly, when one's life is in jeopardy, secondly, when one is in a desperate state on account of illness or death, and thirdly, when one is conscious of sin or guilt. And he explained that these three seem to have their source in human weakness.

Seeing such human weaknesses deeply rooted in our

minds, Honen, the founder of Pure Land Buddhism in Japan, found the solution in the Nembutsu. Honen said, "In Buddhism there are eighty four thousand teachings which are all of worthy recognition, but to me the one that suits me best is the teaching of the Nembutsu." No matter how important a teaching may be: if it is absorbed only by the educated and not by the uneducated; or if it is accomplished by the rich and not by the poor; or if it is observed by the virtuous and not by the sinful; or if it is understood by the adult and not the youngster; if these were the case, then the teaching would only be appreciated by a small fraction of the people. This can never be called the teaching of true salvation for all. On the other hand, the recitation of the Nembutsu does not make any distinction whatever or wherever we may be. It can be recited by all people regardless of race, color or sex. This teaching of the Nembutsu was first discovered by Honen among the eight million and four thousand teachings of Buddhism.

Honen was born in 1133 around the time the Crusaders began to march toward Israel to recapture the Holy Land in the West. He was the son of a samurai in the Province of Mimasaka, about 100 miles west of Kyoto, Japan. In those days, Japan was in a critical condition as a result of a series of civil wars which occured one after another. Samurai were fighting each other and revenge was openly permitted among themselves.

When Honen was only eight years old, his father, Tokikuni, was abruptly murdered one dark night by his enemies. Honen immediately wished for vengeance, but at his father's death-bed he was persuaded by his father to forgive the slayers. Honen was told by his dying father, "You should not be revengeful, because should you be so, other vengeances are bound to follow, and the cycle of evil will never cease." Hearing those last words from his father, Honen, though he was young, decided to become a Buddhist novice. When he became thirteen years old, he went up to Mt. Hiei, the learning Mecca of Japanese Buddhism, to study the teaching of Lord Buddha. So diligently did he study that soon he became one of the cleverest monks on the mountain. His master one day told him that he would become the archbishop of the sect, but Honen simply said that he would instead become a true monk to save himself and the suffering people roaming the streets.

In those days, the truth of Buddhism was said to be acquired through the observance of secret rites or the mechanical recitation of holy scriptures. The monks on Mt. Hiei were, on the other hand, desperately corrupt and attracted by the pursuit of fame and luxury. The people were mostly attracted by the grandeur of Buddhist art represented by glorious images, statues, paintings and ornaments of the Buddha. Strongly dissatisfied with these phenomena, Honen himself tried to reevaluate the Buddhist truth through his own experience. He firmly believed that the Buddhist truth should be simple and direct to appeal to the very heart of man, whoever he might be. Therefore, after putting strenuous efforts into his studies of Pure Land Buddhism, particularly of Shan-tao, he finally came to the conclusion that everyone, since he had a potential Buddha-nature, should be saved by the Amida Buddha if he had a firm faith in Him. In order to gain such faith, no knowledge about Him was necessary. The practice of Nembutsu, the ever-renewing concentration on the Name of Amida Buddha only, was required. He, therefore, moved down to Yoshimizu for the initiation of his new way of life, and expounded it openly in the streets of Kyoto, then the capital of Japan. Because of his active missionary work, the new gospel stirred strong opposition from the traditional Buddhist circles and court nobles who were at ease relying on the authority of a worldly order. As his gospel rapidly spread among the people of all classes, the propagation of Nembutsu was finally banned by the Imperial Order.

Honen never hesitated to spread the gospel. One night he had a strange dream about himself. He was travelling alone on the plains toward the west, and all of a sudden there appeared two rivers. One was a river of fire on his right, and the other was a river of water on his left. They seemed bottomless and wide, and right between these two rivers ran a narrow path of four or five inches wide. Although the two banks were separated by a short distance, it was too dangerous to pass. When he turned around he saw tigers and wolves rushing toward him. Fearing death, he was in a dreadful predicament, and in the meantime a voice came from ahead of him, saying, "Come here, or else you will die." He decided to go ahead single-heartedly, and as he proceeded he arrived safely at the western bank, the land of beauty and purity. A gentle monk was waiting there for him. This monk was called Shan-tao, the great teacher of Jodo Buddhism in China. As he was pleased to see him, Shantao gripped his hand, and Honen finally awakened from the dream. This story shows that man as a lonely traveller has to cross the narrow path of human conscience looking at the rivers of passion and greed on both sides. He always listens to the voice of Amida Buddha before him and the secular human voices behind him. Therefore, it symbolizes the fate of human life which everyone of us is obliged to accept.

Greatly encouraged by the dream, Honen expounded the gospel with a firm conviction led by the voice of Amida Buddha. Many hundreds of thousands of people converted into his fold despite the prohibition, and the government consequently took a firm action to banish him. Honen was exiled to the isle of Shikoku in 1207 when he was seventy-four years old. He willingly accepted this fate believing that his exile would allow him to preach the gospel in a far region where none of the inhabitants would have heard of it as yet. On his way to exile, one of the Government officials who unwillingly persecuted him because of the order sent him off with a poem:

> Though pitiful is the parting
> At the bridge that everyone must pass
> How regretful I am to make you cross.

Honen replied with his own poem:

> Although our bodies are perishable
> Like dew drops melting here and there

Our minds are as one—
Lying on the same flowerbed.

Accompanied by his few disciples, Honen left Kyoto and crossed the rugged ocean to the isle of Shinkoku where he never tired of preaching the gospel even to the fishermen. One day when he looked upon the autumn moon hanging over the pine trees, he murmured a poem which later became the Jodo Mission anthem:

There is no place where the moonlight
Casts not its ray cheering and bright
For us who have the awakened eye
That light will always be cheering and bright.

Imagine the sentiment of a man who is exiled in a far land looking up at the same moon which he saw in his home town! Honen, however, had a strong conviction despite the hardships he met during his exile. He was always encouraged by recalling the following passage found in the scripture: "Though the people throw clods of dirt or sticks at me, I will go on preaching, feeling no hatred toward them, because they simply do not understand me." People are usually in despair when they are insulted and tend to lose their temper because of anger. However, for Honen, the more hardships he met the more he felt the saving power of Amida Buddha and became serene because of his strong faith in Him.

Four years later Honen was pardoned because of a

change in governement and was brought back to Kyoto again. After he returned from his exile, he preached the gospel more than ever though his health declined day by day. His disciples worried about him, and one day one of his disciples asked him, "Do you think everyone of us will surely be born in the Land of Bliss after death?" He answered, "Surely, all who came from the Land of Bliss are going to return to the same place." His disciples began to realize that the master's death was approaching, and they asked him, "To all famous masters were dedicated memorial temples, but no such temple has ever been built for you. Where, then, should we build one?" Honen replied, "If you erect a memorial to me, the influence of my teaching will be confined to one place, and not widely spread. The only thing that you can do for me is to spread the new gospel far and wide. Wherever the spirit of Nembutsu is found, there is my memorial temple."

On January 23, as Honen was requested on his sickbed to summarize the essence of his teaching, he took up a brush and wrote the *Ichimai Kishomon* (One Sheet Document). It is as follows:

"By Nembutsu I do not mean the practice of meditation on the Buddha as is referred to by the wise men of China and Japan, nor is it the invocation of the Buddha's name, which is practiced as the result of study and understanding of the meaning of Nembutsu. It is just to invoke the name of Amida, without doubting that this will issue in the rebirth of the believer in the Pure Land. Just this, and no other considerations are

required. Mention is often made of the threefold heart
and the four manners of exercise, but these are all included in the belief that rebirth in the Pure Land is
most conclusively assured by the Namu Amida Butsu.
If one imagines something more than this, one will be
excluded from the blessings of the two Holy Ones,
Amida and Shakyamuni, and left out of the Original
Vow. Those who believe in the Nembutsu, however
learn through in all the teachings of Shakyamuni that
they should behave themselves like ignoramuses who
know nothing, or like simple-hearted women-devotees:
avoiding pedantry, and invoking the Buddha's name
with singleness of heart."

Honen firmly believed that there is no other way
leading to the salvation of all men except by the way of
Nembutsu, the concentration on the Name of Amida
Buddha and its application in our daily life. His discovery
of a new way of life which is applicable to all men, is
unique in our human history. On the 25th of January,
1212, at the age of eighty, Honen, surrounded by his disciples, kept repeating the Nembutsu till his strength
failed him. As he drew near the end, he put on the robe
and lay down with his head to the north, and his face
toward the west, and recited the following passage from
the scripture: "May the light of Amida Buddha illumine
the whole world so that those who call upon the Nembutsu will be saved and never forsaken." His voice of
calling the Nembutsu became weaker and weaker, then
hushed all together.

Honen's departure took place at noon. It was so peaceful and calm that no one knew when he took his last breath. While he was alive, he used to recall Shan-tao's message, "O my disciples, when you are at the final moment, I wish you to make your minds unruffled, unconfused, and undespaired. Always make your mind and body straight and pleasant, and concentrate yourself unto the Name of Amida Buddha." His gentle face smiling, he finally realized his life long wish at his very departure. Though the lips of the saint were silent forever, and a long time has elapsed since he passed away, his teaching has become more and more widely spread among the people who desperately need salvation in this world.

Honen's wish was carried out by his disciples, and the one regarded as topmost to have elaborated the teaching of Honen and Pure Land Buddhism, is Shinran. He was born in 1173 in the province of Hino near Kyoto, as the son of Lord Hino. When he was nine years of age, he became a Buddhist apprentice and went up to Mt. Hiei to study Buddhism. However, like his master Honen, he could not be satisfied with the existing teaching, and after some twenty years of study there, he decided to leave. He went down to Yoshimizu where he became a disciple of Honen in 1201. He was spiritually awakened through Honen's cordial guidance, and he stood bravely on the firm rock of faith. He assisted his master Honen in all possible ways in spreading the teaching of Nembutsu. Because of the popularity of Nembutsu among the masses of people, which however stirred the jealousy of the monks of the traditional denominations, Honen and Shinran, together with other disciples, were deprived of their ecclesiastical orders, given secular names, and sentenced to exile in 1207: Honen to the isle of Shikoku and Shinran to Echigo, in the northern part of Japan. From that time on, Shinran declared that he was neither a monk nor a layman. That is to say, he could enjoy the free position of a real truth seeker, although he was still an honest follower of Buddhism. During his exile, he was believed to have married Esshin-ni.

Honen and Shinran were both pardoned from exile on the same day in 1211, and Shinran headed for the Kanto regions instead of returning to Kyoto. He stayed mostly in Ibaragi Prefecture, preaching the Nembutsu for twenty years there. He wrote his famous work, *the Kyogyo Shinsho* (Analects concerning Doctrine, Practice, Faith and Attainment) refuting the traditional Buddhist teachings while collecting passages from the sutras and commentaries to support his standpoint. Around the age of sixty, Shinran and his family appear to have returned to Kyoto and to have lived in Nembutsu until he passed away in 1262 at the age of ninty.

It is interesting to note that both Honen and Shinran lost their parents while they were young, and had gone through bitter life experiences which accounted for the awakening of their faith. Both of them were also accutely aware of their passion-ridden nature and impossibility of purifying their spirit, without the assurance of enlightenment and rebirth into the Pure Land given by Amida Buddha. They solely relied on their masters; Honen to

Shan-tao, and Shinran to Honen, respectively. Honen
once said, "I, who have followed the teachings of Shan-
tao in accordance with Genshin, have been repeating
the Nembutsu over six thousand times a day, and since
I have come nearer to life's close, I have added ten thousand more, and made it seventy thousand times a day."
Shinran said, "As for me, there is nothing left except to
believe in the guidance of the teaching of the Venerable
Master: 'We are saved by Amida merely through reciting
the Nembutsu alone'. I, myself, do not know, after all,
whether the Nembutsu is truly the cause of rebirth in the
Pure Land, or whether it is the Karma to make us sink
into the bottomless pit. I shall never regret my belief to
recite the Nembutsu even if I am deceived by the Venerable Honen, and fall into the bottomless pit." The above
mentioned passages clearly indicated how Honen and
Shinran devoted themselves to the teaching of their
masters, and this feeling of absolute dependence is
essential to anyone who is earnestly seeking salvation.

Although they have standpoints in common, there are
some differences in their understanding of salvation. For
Honen, the practice of repeating the Nembutsu is considered to be a means to attain the goal of salvation. For
Shinran, the perspective is entirely reversed, namely, all
spiritual benefit comes from Amida Buddha and He
alone is the source of virtue and merit. For Shinran, the
recitation of Nembutsu is the expression of gratitude, and
when we have this faith, salvation is assured. Honen
paved the way for the growth of popular Pure Land
thought to make clear that the practice of recitation is

the most suitable means of practice for the masses of people in the degenerated age. Shinran gave the theological meaning to this practice, saying that the act of faith itself is the essential basis of salvation and was not made by the individual, but by Amida Buddha alone.

Their teachings were crystallized in the form of denominations such as the Jodo and the Jodo Shin sects of Japanese Buddhism as seen today, and which have attracted more than half of the entire Japanese population. The secret of their rapid growth in Japanese religious history is due to the fact that the majority of the Japanese are of the schizoid type who, unlike Westerners, are passive, flexible, tolerable, undemonstrative, emotional, sensitive, feminine, suggestive, naive, aesthetic and so on. They are easily attracted to the simple and direct teaching of Nembutsu which assures salvation for the common people who are neglected and barred by their social situations from entering into the rigorous monastic life or attending expensive and mysterious rites. I really do not know which comes first just like the chicken or the egg, namely, because of the schizoid type of the Japanese character they are easily attracted by the Pure Land thought, or because of the Pure Land thought they retain harmony within and always eager to absorb something new and valuable from outside and enrich their culture throughout the ages. One thing which is certain is that both elements are intermingled with each other and formed the Japanese spirituality.

It is also noted that the Japanese have been imbued with the shamanistic elements of folk religion. Professor

Ichiro Hori pointed out that one of the main social functions of Japanese Buddhism on the common level has been religious services for spirits of the dead as well as for divine favors in this world. When someone died, the Nembutsu was recited by the people for the protection of the corpse, and for early rebirth into Amida's Pure Land. During the period of mourning, which lasted for seven weeks, there was incessant repeating of the name of Amida in a memorial service. The Buddhist priests sometimes played an important role as mediator to console the soul of the dead on behalf of the bereaved families. Although several Pure Lands were advocated by the eminent Buddhist monks in the pre-Kamakura period, and other invocations, like "Namu Daishi Henjo Kongo" and "Namu Myoho Rengekyo" were initiated by Kukai and Nichiren respectively, the Amida's Pure Land and the Nembutsu occupied the predominant position among the Japanese people.

We cannot, however, take these views phenomenally. The Pure Land is not the geographical area which is supposed to be situated in the west and reserved for the departed, but is the content of salvation for the devotees. The Nembutsu has no connotation of magical efficacy or merit. It is the thorough recitation of "Namu Amida Butsu", which means the adoration to Amida Buddha of infinite Light and Life. "Namu" literally means "I take refuge" which is the subject of faith, and "Amida Butsu", the object of worship. It signifies the union of subject and object in a dynamic sense. Therefore, by means of practicing the Nembutsu, we shall become one with Amida

Buddha and finally attain the Oneness of life. Here, selfish efforts are totally annihilated: the decision in every act is not made according to our own judgment but only by and with Amida Buddha. He is the guiding light and the voice of conscience which come from the transcendental Other, and only through deep confidence in Him, can we see our true selves and attain a clear understanding of ourselves and the universe.

When we think that no one can save us but Amida Buddha, the Nembutsu comes out in our voices. When we fully understand that there is no place for calm resignation and we cannot lie idle for a moment, the Nembutsu of warning comes to our lips. And when we realize that we owe much to others, the Nembutsu of gratitude springs up. In this way, the Nembutsu is the fountainhead of all joy; when we are in a desperate state, it becomes the means of relief; when we are living in idleness it becomes the means of encouragement for the better life, and, when we are blessed with good fortune, it becomes a manifestation of gratitude.

Everyone is seeking happiness, and no one wants to suffer. Setting aside all the sufferings which confront us, and progressing toward the ultimate happiness, is the way we should tread, and this is the way the Jodo Mission is teaching in the Nembutsu, the most accessible and simplest means for the betterment of ourselves and our world.

*The front picture shows the image of Bodhisattva Ashura en-
shrined at Kohukuji Temple in Nara.*

Chapter 2

Jodo Mission Service Order

THE ORDER OF GENERAL SERVICE

1. Koge (Call to worship)
   We wish to purify our body with incense smoke
   And to make our minds as the fire of Wisdom.
   With every moment of aspiration, we wish
   To dedicate ourselves to the Infinite and
   Boundless Buddha.

2. Sanborai (Three Refuges)
   With a concentrated heart we put our trust
   in the Buddha.
   With a concentrated heart we put our trust
   in the Dharma.
   With a concentrated heart we put our trust
   in the Samgha.

3. Shibujo (Invocation)
   We earnestly wish that the Tathagata of the ten
   directions, Shakyamuni Buddha, Amida Buddha,
   and the Bodhisattvas Kannon and Seishi, be
   present here in this holy place.

4. Tanbutsuge (Aspiration)

> The body of the Tathagata is marvelous
> And nothing is comparable to His miraculous Power.
> Now we reverently take refuge in Him.
> The form of the Tathagata is immortal
> And his Wisdon prevails as the Dharma is imminent.
> Now we reverently take refuge in Him.

5. Ryakusange (Confession)

> We wish to confess our past deeds
> Which were full of ignorance and greed.
> We wish to dedicate our whole heart
> To the Saving Power of Amida Buddha.

6. Junen (Calling the name of Amida Buddha ten times)

7. Kaikyoge (Prelude to the Scripture chanting)

> Nothing is comparable to the Wonderful Teaching revealed by the Buddha. It is hardly given to us, and yet we are now to receive it. We aspire to the true meaning of the Buddha's Teaching.

8. Shiseige (The Three Bodhissattva's Vows)

> We wish to take unlimited vows
> So that the Highest Truth can be attained
> Should these vows not be fulfilled
> We shall not gain Perfect Enlightenement.

Should we not for infinite kalpas
Become great nor offer help
And save those in need
We shall not gain Perfect Enlightenment.

When we attain the Highest Truth
The Buddha's Compassion will permeate to all
beings
Should there be anyone who receives it not
We shall not gain Perfect Enlightenment.

Refrain from craving, and may pure thought
penetrate
Our minds, we should attain
The Highest Truth always anew
Which leads to Perfect Enlightenment.

With courage the miracle comes
Which shall brighten the whole world,
Thereby we shall eliminate the illusions
And save those in despair.

Let us keep our eyes open
In order that the darkness be cleared
Let us lead the Good Life
In order that the evil paths be closed.

When we attain the Highest Truth
Peace prevails in all directions.
The Sun and Moon will seek the darkness

And natural light will be diminished.

Now let us reveal the Buddha's world
So that we shall share the Buddha's merits
Among the people we will always
Expound the way like a lion's cry.

We take refuge in all the Buddhas
To whom the virtues are bestowed.
When we follow the Buddha's Way
We shall become as the king of kings.

The Buddha is the Perfect Knower
Shining bright with infinite Love.
We wish our deeds to shine
Like our Lord Buddha, the Exalted One.

When our vows are all fulfilled
Sentient beings shall rejoice.
The heavens will be adorned with beautiful flow-
ers
Like a shower in full scent.

9.   Eko (Dedication)

All this chanting of scripture is respectfully dedicated to those who hear it so that they may be
born into the Pure Land.

10. Junen (Calling the name of Amida Buddha ten
times.)

11. Shoyakumon (Invocation)

> May the light of Amida Buddha illumine the whole world so that all sentient beings can be saved and never forsaken.

12. Nembutsu-ichie (Penetration into the Name of Buddha)

13. Soekomon (Final Dedication)

> By virtue of calling the name of Amida Buddha,
> May all sentient beings have the Buddha's mind,
> And be born into the Pure Land.

14. Junen (Calling the name of Amida Buddha ten times.)

15. Go-hogo (Recitation of Honen's message)

16. Junen (Calling the name of Amida Buddha ten times)

17. Shiguseigan (The Bodhisattva's Vows)

> However innumerable are sentient beings,
> We earnestly wish to save them all.
> However inexhaustible are the passions,
> We earnestly wish to extinguish them all.
> However immeasurable are the teachings,
> We earnestly wish to understand them all.

> We sincerely hope that we can prove the

Truth of Buddhism.
We sincerely hope that we can share the
Truth with others.
We sincerely hope that we shall attain
Buddhahood.

18. Sanjinrai (Three Refuges)

We put our trust in Amida Buddha
Who has accomplished His great vows,
In order to attain the Pure Land.
We put our trust in Amida Buddha
Who has now given us his guiding light,
In order to attain the Pure Land.
We put our trust in Amida Buddha
Who is now receiving us in the Pure Land,
In order to attain the Pure Land.

19. Sobutsuge (Postlude)

Now we wish that the Buddha will return safely to
His Original State.
A reverent offering of incense and flowers, we wish
to send to the Buddha wholeheartedly.
We earnestly wish that the Buddha will protect us
so that we may all together live
in the light of the Buddha's Compassion and
Wisdom.

Chapter 3

Selected Scriptures of the Jodo Mission

THE VERSE ON THE ADORATION OF AMIDA BUDDHA IN THE MURYOJUKYO

His visage shines aloft,
Dignified and divine.
It burns so bright
That none ever equals it.

The splendors of the Sun,
Moon and gems;
They all are hidden
As dark as black ink.

His visage is superior,
And none is comparable
His calling, the voice of Truth
Sounds and resounds to all.

Great is His restraint,
Right effort and Samadhi.
His Wisdom is so rare
That none is like Him.

Deeply He sees the universe
And clearly perceives in it
The great ocean of Truth,
Its width and depth He finds.

In Him dwells no ignorance,
Greed nor anger,
Boldly like a lion He preaches,
And his power is boundless.

His merit is unlimited,
And His Wisdom is profound.
His light permeates far and wide,
And the universe trembles.

Would that we excel in
Giving, balancing in life,
Restraint and forbearance;
Rewarding will be such deeds.

For the attainment of Buddhahood
We will fulfill our wishes,
Overcoming our fears,
And peace will prevail.

Hundreds of thousands
Of billions of Buddhas dwell
Who are as many as the sands
Of the river Ganges.

Instead of dedicating
To them, we wish to tread
The way unswervingly,
Without going astray.

Too numerous to count
Are the Buddha's worlds
Like counting the sands
Of the river Ganges.

When we become Buddhas
our light shines throughout the universe.
Thus we try to make ourselves
dignified and holy.

Let the other Buddhas shine
Throughout the whole universe
they reign to make the people
holy and to purify their minds.

Wishing to attain the Bodhi
As our Buddha did,
Beyond our life we go.
Enlightenment is our goal.

All beings are welcome
To have pleasure and serenity.
When they reach our land
Happiness and Peace prevail.

Our Buddha be the witness
And trust our wishes,
In His concern we strive
To save all beings.

We shall make our land
As the land of Nirvana
And pity those who suffer
Enabling them to be enlightened.

O, the Buddhas of all lands,
The containers of Wisdom.
Protect our noble wishes
Until we fulfill them.

Even if we are full of pain
Which tortures us cruelly,
We shall dare to endure
And will never complain.

လ လ လ

THE CHAPTER ON THE ADORATION OF AMIDA BUDDHA IN THE MURYOJUKYO

Thus the Buddha said to Ananda: "The Light that issues from Amida Buddha is most brilliant, and none is comparable to Him. Therefore we also call on Him in adoration:

the Buddha of Infinite Light, the Buddha of Boundless

Light, the Buddha of Unhindered Light, the Buddha of Incomparable Light, the Buddha of Burning Light, the Buddha of Pure Light, the Buddha of Joyous Light, the Buddha of Wisdom's Light, the Buddha of Incessant Light, The Buddha of Unthinkable Light, the Buddha of Inexpressible Light, and the Buddha whose Light surpasses the Sun and the Moon.

Anyone who is blessed with this Light will get rid of his filthy mind; his body will be at ease, and rejoicing goodness will come. Should anyone meet this Light in his despair, he will be restful with no pain and will obtain enlightenment when he passes away. The Light of Amida Buddha is in full splendor, and shines over the whole universe. Not only do I adore His Light, but also adore Him. If anyone, on receiving the great virtues of this Light, adores Him day and night incessantly and sincerely in his heart, he will naturally be born into His Pure Land, and his exercises will be highly adorned by all the bodhisattvas, shravakas and people. When he is born and embraced with the light of bodhi, his virtue will be highly adorned by all the Buddhas and bodhisattvas of the universe alike."

The Buddha further said: "Even though I adore the magnificence of Amida Buddha day and night, I may not be able to describe Him well."

෩ ෩ ෩

THE CHAPTER ON THE
CONTEMPLATION OF AMIDA BUDDHA
IN THE KANMURYOJUKYO

The Buddha said to Ananda and Vaidehi: "When you achieve this perception, you should then contemplate the bodily marks and the Light of Amida Buddha. Know, Ananda, that the body of Amida Buddha is hundreds of thousands of millions times as bright as the color of the Jambudana gold of the heavenly Yama! The height of that Buddha is six billion nayutas of yojanas as innumerable as the sands of the river Ganges. The white eyelashes are twisted to the right, and they look like five Sumeru Mountains. The Buddha's eyes are like the great Ocean and shine brilliantly. Through the pores of His body are sent forth lights which look like Mount Sumeru. The halo of the Buddha is like ten thousand millions of the three thousand million worlds. And in that halo there are transformed Buddhas numbering ten billion nayutas as innumerable as the sands of the river Ganges. Each of these Buddhas has numerous numbers of transformed bodhisattvas for attendants. Amida Buddha has eighty-four thousand signs and marks. Each mark has eighty-four thousand lights, and each light shines over the whole universe. All beings who contemplate the Buddha will be saved and never be forsaken. The lights issuing from Him, the marks and signs of Amida Buddha and the transformed Buddhas: they are all beyond explanation. Only through our contemplation are we able to see them. One who sees them will at once perceive all the Buddhas of the universe. Therefore, we call this state Samadhi, the Oneness of Life. Those who have attained this state are able to contemplate the bodies of the Buddhas. Since they contemplate on the Buddha's body, they can perceive the Buddha's mind, namely, the Great Compassion. With His Compassion, the Buddha saves all beings. Those who have exercised this contemplation will, when the next life comes, be born in the Buddha's world, and gain everlasting life. Therefore, the wise should direct their thoughts to Amida Buddha.

"Those who wish to perceive Amida Buddha should begin with one single sign or mark. You could first contemplate one of His white eyelashes as clearly as possible. As it appears, the eighty-four thousand signs and marks will be seen. Once you see Amida Buddha, you will see all the innumerable numbers of Buddhas in the universe. Since you are able to see them, you will be qualified as a Buddha-to-be in the presence of the Buddha.

"This is the perception gained by the contemplation on the forms and bodies of the Buddha and is called the Ninth Contemplation. The exercise of this contemplation is right and any other exercise is heretical."

လ လ လ

THE SCRIPTURE IN
THE PRAISE OF
AMIDA BUDDHA'S PARADISE

Thus I have heard: At one time the Buddha dwelt at Shravasti, staying in the Jetavana garden of Anathapindada. He was accompanied by twelve hundred and fifty bhikshus who were well known for their great wisdom. They were Shariputra the Elder, Mahamaudgalydyana, Mahakashyapa, Mahakatyayana, Mahakaushthilya, Revata, Shudhipanthaka, Nanda, Ananda, Rahula, Gavampati, Pindolabharadvaja, Kalodayin, Mahakapphina, Vakkula, Aniruddha, and other disciples. There were also such bodhisattvas as Manjushri, Ajita, Ghandhahahastin, Nityadyukta and an innumerable number of such devas as Shakra and others.

Then the Buddha said to Shariputra the Elder: "There is a world called Paradise in the west beyond the ten billion Buddha worlds, where lives Amida Buddha to preach the noble teaching. We call this world Paradise, because there is no suffering and sorrow. Instead it is full of pleasure and happiness.

"And in this Paradise there are seven rows of balustrades, fine nets and roadside trees which are decorated with four gems, namely, gold, silver, emerald, and crystal. Therefore, we call it Paradise.

"And in this Paradise there are seven ponds filled with water of eight qualities. The beds of the ponds are paved with golden sand, and the stairs on the four sides are made of gold, silver, emerald, and crystal. Up above are towers and palaces which are decorated with gold, silver, emerald, crystal, clam, red pearl, and agate. In the ponds are lotus flowers which are as large as chariot wheels. The blue lotus flowers shine blue, yellow ones shine yellow, red ones shine red, white ones shine white and they all evaporate their fragrance completely. So this Paradise is fully adorned with excellent qualities.

"And in this Paradise heavenly music is played at all times. On the golden land is poured mandarava flowers six times each day and night. In the cool morning, the people of this world carry their flower vessels with beautiful flowers, and make offerings to the ten billion Buddhas of all directions. At noon they come back home and take meals and stroll. So this Paradise is fully adorned with excellent qualities.

"And in this Paradise there are a number of beautiful birds such as swans, peacocks, parrots, sharikas, kalavinkas, and jivamjivakas. They sing in melodious tones six times each day and night, proclaiming the Law of the Five Virtues, the Five Powers, the Seven Steps towards the Awakened Mind, and the Noble Eightfold Paths. Hearing these tunes, the people in this world take refuge in the Buddha, Dharma and Samgha. You should not think that these birds are the transfigurations of past karma. In this world the Three Realms do not exist nor is there any notion of the Three Realms. These birds are nothing but manifestations of Amida Buddha which preach his wonderful teachings.

"O Shariputra, in this world are blown gentle breezes

which bring about wonderful tunes as they move the roadside trees and the fine nets of gems. It is like a hundred thousand tunes played all at once, so the people hearing this music take refuge in the Buddha, Dharma and Samgha. O Shariputra, so this Paradise is fully adorned with excellent qualities.

"O Shariputra, what do you think the reason we call Amida Buddha? O Shariputra, the Buddha's light is boundless and shines over the ten quarters without hindrance. So, we call him Amida Buddha.

"And, O Shariputra, the life of that Buddha and his people is also immeasurable. So, we call him Amida Buddha. O Shariputra, already ten kalpas have passed since he attained Buddhahood. And, O Shariputra, Buddha is accompanied by an innumerable number of shravaka and bodhisattva disciples. O Shariputra, so this Paradise is fully adorned with excellent qualities.

"And, O Shariputra, the people who are reborn in this world attain the unretrogressive state. Among them are a countless number of already attained Bodhisattvas who have been in existence throughout the ages.

"O Shariputra, whosoever hears this wonderful teaching should abandon his selfish efforts and make a vow in order to be born into this world. They can be met by other aspiring people in this world. O Shariputra, one cannot be born into this world with small virtues.

"O Shariputra, if a good man or woman, hearing Amida Buddha's teaching, bear his Name for one, two, three, four, five, six, or seven days with a single mind, Amida Buddha accompanied with his attendants will appear before him at the moment of passing away from this mundane world. Then, without hindrance, one can be immediately born into Amida Buddha's world of Paradise.

"O Shariputra, I proclaim this teaching because I know its legitimacy. Therefore, those who hear my teaching and wish to be born into this world should make a vow to Amida Buddha.

"O Shariputra, as I praise the innumerable virtues of Amida Buddha, there are also in the East a countless number of Buddhas such as Buddha Akshobhya, Merudhvaja, Mahameru, Meruprabhasa, Manjudhvaja, and others who proclaim to the world; 'Ye, believe in this noble teaching which praises the innumerable virtues of Amida Buddha and which all Buddhas protect and aspire to.'

"O Shariputra, there are also in the South, a countless number of Buddhas such as Buddha Chandrasuryapradipa, Yashahprabha, Maharchiskandha, Merupradipa, Anantavirya, and others who proclaim to the world; 'Ye, believe in this noble teaching which praises the innumerable virtues of Amida Buddha and which all Buddhas protect and aspire to.'

"O Shariputra, there are also in the West, a countless number of Buddhas such as Buddha Amitayus, Amitaskandha, Amitadhvaja, Mahaprabha, Mahanirbhasa, Maharatnaketu, Shuddharashmiprabha and others who proclaim to the world; 'Ye, believe in this noble teaching which praises the innumerable vitues of Amida Buddha and which all Buddhas protect and aspire to.'

"O Shariputra, there are also in the North, a countless number of Buddhas such as Buddha Maharchiskandha, Vaishvanaranirghosa, Dushpradharsha, Adityasambhava, Jeleniprabha, and others who proclaim to the world, 'Ye, believe in this noble teaching which praises the innumerable virtues of Amida Buddha and which all Buddhas protect and aspire to.'

"O Shariputra, there are also in the Nadir a countless number of Buddhas such as Buddha Shinha, Yashas, Yashahprabhasa, Dharma, Dharmadhvaja, Dharmadhara and others who proclaim to the world; 'Ye believe in this noble teaching which praises the innumerable virtues of Amida Buddha and which all Buddhas protect and aspire to.'

"O Shariputra, there are also in the Zenith a countless number of Buddhas such as Buddha Brahmaghosha, Nakshatraraja, Gaudhottamo, Gandhaprabhasa, Maharchiskandha, Ratnakusumasampushpitagatra, Salendraraja, Ratnatpalashri, Sarvarthadarsha, Sumerukalpa, and others who proclaim to the world; 'Ye, believe in this noble teaching which praises the innumerable virtues of Amida Buddha and which all Buddhas protect and aspire to.'

"O Shariputra, for what reason do you think we call this noble teaching which praises the innumerable virtues of Amida Buddha and which all Buddhas protect and aspire to? Because a good man or woman who hears the Name and the teaching of Amida Buddha will in turn be protected and aspired to by all Buddhas and will attain the highest Peace and Happiness without falling back. Therefore, O Shariputra, believe in my word and the teachings of all the Buddhas.

"O Shariputra, those who wished, wish or will wish to be born into this Amida Buddha's world will attain the highest Peace and Happiness and never fall back. They are already born, or are now being born, or shall be born in the near future into this world. Therefore, O Shariputra, those good men or women who believe in my teaching should make a vow and be born into this world.

"O Shariputra, as I praise the inconceivable virtues of all Buddhas, they also praise my inconceivable virtues, saying, 'Shakyamuni Buddha has well accomplished a rare thing of extreme difficulty and attained the highest Peace and Happiness in this wicked world of five corruptions; namely, the corruptions of age, idea, human nature, fellowship, and life. After having attained the highest Peace and Happiness, he preached the noble teaching for the sake of saving all sentient beings.'

"O Shariputra, remember that in this wicked world of five corruptions, I have achieved the highest Peace and Happiness and preach the noble teaching for the sake of saving all sentient beings. It is the most difficult and yet the most meaningful thing to do."

When the Buddha finished his sermon, Shariputra and all the bhikshus, devas, men, and asuras applauded his speech, and after paying homage to the Buddha, they left the scene rejoicing.

☙ ☙ ☙

THE SCRIPTURE CONCERNING
THE TRUE STATE OF BEING

Hannya Haramita Shingyo

When the Bodhisattva was in deep meditation, he clearly perceived that the five components of being are all Sunya and so he was saved from all kinds of suffering.

(Then he said to Shariputra) "O Shariputra! Phenomena are not different from Sunya and Sunya is not different from phenomena. Phenomena are Sunya and Sunya is phenomena.

"O Shariputra, all is Sunya. Nothing comes into existence nor passes out of existence. There is no purity and no impurity; no increase nor decrease. Therefore, in Sunya there is no form, no sensation, no thought, no volition, no perception; there is no eye, ear, nose, tongue, body, mind; and there is no form, sound, odor, taste, touch, nor consciousness. There is neither field of vision nor field of thought and consciousness.

"In Sunya there is no ignorance and no extinction of ignorance. There is neither decay nor death; nor is there termination of decay and death; there is no suffering, no source of suffering, nor annihilation of suffering, and no way to the annihilation of suffering.

"In Sunya there is no knowledge, likewise no attainment in knowledge as there is nothing to attain.

"The mind of the Bodhisattva which has found its source in the Prajna Paramita is without hindrances and he has no fear. Going beyond all hindrances and illusions he reaches Perfect Enlightenment.

"All the Buddhas of the past, present and future have found their source in the Prajna Paramita; they have found Perfect Enlightenment."

Therefore, we know that the Prajna Paramita is the Great Gatha, the Gatha of Great Wisdom, the Supreme Gatha, the unequaled Gatha which is capable of removing all suffering.

Because of its truth, we make known the Prajna Paramita Gatha which is:

Strive, strive constantly towards the goal of Perfect Wisdom, Sowaka (So may it be)!

Chapter 4

Explanation of Buddhist Services

WHEN YOUR CHILD IS BORN

On the seventh day after the birth of a child, a family feast known as the *oshichiya* is held. The first service called the "Tri-Ratna Service" is held on the 100th day or thereafter at the church with the new born baby and parents attending. The baby is blessed by the Buddha for taking of refuge in the Three Treasures (Buddha, Dharma, and Samgha) and having become one of His children.

જી જી જી

CONFIRMATION CEREMONY

When we become mature and independent we are taken in front of the main altar of the church to express our sincere reliance upon the Buddha, and to pledge ourselves to follow the teachings of Buddhism. This ceremony is usually held at a special anniversary service or when the Chief Abbot is in attendance. Sometimes on this day we are given a white cotton cloth on which is written the name of Amida Buddha.

જી જી જી

WHEN WE GET MARRIED

The date and time of a wedding ceremony should be discussed with the minister in advance, and premarital counselling may be requested at the church. Rehearsal is conducted prior to the wedding ceremony. You are asked to bring your marriage license issued by the Board of Health, and to be accompanied by your attendants including your parents, maid of honor, bride's maids, best man, ushers, flower girl or ring bearer at this time. On the wedding day the ceremony is solemnly initiated with the vow to the Buddha followed by the wedding procession. After the offering of incense to the Buddha, you are asked to receive purified water by the officiating minister. The *juzu*, the Buddhist rosary, is given to you as the testimony of marriage before the Buddha, and a pledge is exchanged for the confirmation of your marriage. After the minister's pronouncement of the completion of your wedding ceremony, you are asked to retire from the church hall with the other attendants. This is the end of the Buddhist wedding ceremony.

Getting married is easy, but staying married is hard. In order to lead a happy wedded life, mutual understanding and adjustment are required. Both husband and wife should "give in" gracefully, not grudgingly, and solve their problems cooperatively whatever they may be. Success in marriage demands that you recognize your individual role and that you also recognize and accept the role of the other person. This mutual understanding and adjustment are made possible through the life of the

Nembutsu, a life in harmony with the Buddha and reality.

ɷ ɷ ɷ

ENSHRINEMENT CEREMONY

When we enshrine a new image of Buddha or a new family altar (*butsudan*) at home, we invite a minister to officiate in a short but solemn service. It is also held when a new tombstone, a house, etc. are completed in order to instill the Buddha's spirit into them.

ɷ ɷ ɷ

DEDICATION CEREMONY (KUYO)

In order to pay our last respects to our deceased pets or favorite utensils, which are out of use, we hold a dedication ceremony called *Kuyo* with the minister officiating. The ceremony is held in order that the items may rest in peace after they are discharged from active use.

ɷ ɷ ɷ

WHEN SOMEONE DIES

When someone dies at home, we must report immediately to the church and the mortuary. This eternal farewell is a painful reality, but we must endure it bravely in order to prepare for the funeral service. According to the Buddhist sutra, "the dead body must be cleansed with hot water, dressed in cotton cloth, placed in a coffin,

sprinkled with ointment, covered with aromatics, burned in a fire, and the bones collected and placed in a casket."
Before the deceased is put in a coffin, there is a ceremony called *yukan* (hot water bathing). Formerly, members of the bereaved family, friends, and relatives gathered to watch by the deceased all through the night before the funeral in a service called *Otsuya* (the Wake): but it may be held jointly with the funeral service.

At the funeral service, held either at the church or mortuary, all people concerned are invited along with the ministers who solemnly pay their last respects to the deceased. A Buddhist posthumous name (*kaimyo*) is given to the deceased by the officiating minister to signify the last acceptance of him as a member of the Buddhist fellowship.

ꝏ ꝏ ꝏ

MEMORIAL SERVICES (MEINICHI)

In general the dead body is cremated as Gautama Buddha was, and the ashes are put into the urn which is to be buried under the tombstone or enshrined in the urn room. The *i-hai* (wooden tablet) on which is written the posthumous name, is given to the bereaved family and the 49th day service is reverently observed at the church. It is believed that by the 49th day the karma of the deceased takes a certain form. Thereafter, every year on the day of his death (*Meinichi*) a memorial service is held in memory of the deceased either at the church or at home.

PERPETUAL MEMORIAL SERVICES
(EITAIKYO)

At the request of the bereaved family, the urn may be kept at the church or the *kaimyo* of a deceased kept on file in special church records so that the memorial service can be held for the deceased even though the family may move away or die.

Chapter 5

Explanation of Buddhist Annual Events

~ ~ ~

1. NEHAN-E, THE BUDDHA'S NIRVANA DAY

February 15 is the day of *Nehan* or Parinirvana on which Gautama Buddha passed away from this world about two thousand five hundred years ago. This is a memorable event for all Buddhists in the world just as Christians celebrate Easter in memory of Jesus the Nazarene who was crucified by the Romans in Jerusalem.

Since the Buddha was enlightened under the Bodhi tree at Budhagaya, he never tired of preaching the new way of life. Near Rajagaha, he built a monastery which became one of the most important centers of his activities during the forty-five years of his ministrations. Until the age of eighty years he taught his disciples and the people at large the most appropriate teaching for their needs. One day he received a visitor named Kalamas, a heretic, who decided to become his disciple after hearing of his fame. The Buddha exhorted him, saying, "Now look you, Kalamas. Do not be misled by fame or tradition or hearsay. Do not be misled by the proficiency of sweet words, because they seem becoming, nor by a famous man because he is your teacher. But when you understand thoroughly for yourself that these things are truly good and right and never conducive to loss and sorrow, then accept them." The Buddha strongly opposed his own words being accepted as Truth unless and until they had been proved by application to daily experience.

After a long stay at Rajagaha, he set out on a journey with his five hundred disciples. They visited several villages and towns, and many others followed them. When they stopped at Pava, they were greeted by Chunda, a blacksmith. He offered a meal to them, and everyone enjoyed it. As they had gone only a short distance from Pava, the Buddha suddenly began to feel weary and sick. Ananda, one of his disciples, was surprised and cursed Chunda for having offered the Master a poisonous meal. However, the Buddha said, "Do not blame him as he was unaware of it. Instead, his meal deserves praise since it teaches us the fact that man becomes sick." His disciples were overwhelmed with grief as they knew that their Master's end was drawing near.

When they arrived at Kushinara, a village about 120 miles north-east of Benares, the Buddha asked Ananda to prepare a couch for rest. Ananda spread it under a

Sal-tree where he lay down with his head to the north. It was not the season for flowers to bloom, yet the trees that sheltered the Master were full of flowers. They fell gently upon his couch, and from the sky sweet melodies slowly drifted down. Ananda was weeping and walked away to hide his tears. The Buddha called to him, saying, "Do not grieve and despair. Remember my words: from all that delights us, from all that we love, we must one day be separated. How can that which is born be other than inconstant and perishable? How can that which is created endure forever? You have long honored me. You are faithful to me in thought and in deed. You have done great good; continue in the right path, so that the light of Truth will shine upon you." He further said, "Be islands unto yourselves. Be a refuge to yourself; do not take to yourself any other refuge. Do not seek refuge in anyone but yourself!" "It may be some of you will have the idea: 'The word of the Master is no more, and now we are without a leader.' But, you must not think of it like this. The Teaching of Truth and the Teaching of Fellowship which I have expounded are laid down for you, and let them after I am gone be your Teacher." Then, the Buddha said to his disciples these final words, "This I tell you, my disciples: Decay is inherent in all conditioned things. Work out your own salvation with diligence!"

When the Buddha took his last breath, it has been reported that the earth quivered like a ship struck by a squall, and firebrands fell from the sky. The heavens were lit up by a preternatural fire, which burned without fuel, without smoke, without being fanned by the wind. Fearsome thunderbolts crashed down on the earth, and violent winds raged in the sky. Those who had not gotten rid of their passion shed tears. Most of his disciples lost their composure and felt grief. However, those who remembered well that it is the natural thing to pass away were not shaken from their composure. They recalled the Buddha's instruction that death is an aspect of universal transcience, and only the wise know how to accept its appearance.

The state of the Buddha's passing-away is called Parinirvana which means the complete extinction of personal desire. Affirmatively it is boundless life itself. It is just like the candle-light being blown out. We do not know in what direction the fire has gone, whether to the east, west, north, or south. The Buddha became free of the denotation of "body": he is profound, measureless, unfathomable, even like unto the great ocean.

Usually man fears death and loves life, but when we realize that life is a journey, the beginning and end of which cannot be controlled by ourselves; we cannot simply wait for death that is approaching. Death is rather a harvest of our meaningful life to which we must proceed with diligence. Birth, growth, decay and death are the inevitable cycle of life, and yet to make it meaningful, one must live in the spirit of Buddha of two thousand and five hundred years ago.

ɷ ɷ ɷ

2. HIGAN-E, THE EQUINOX DAY

Higan is the Buddhist festival which falls in March and September for a week. We call the middle of week the vernal and autumnal equinox day respectively meaning that on this day the length of time for day and night is equal. It is the herald of a new season as it says in a Japanese phrase, *"Atsusa samusa mo higan made"* (Until the time of Higan it gets cold or warm). We find in it renewed hope after long weary days of cold or heat.

In all Buddhist temples, the *Higan* service is celebrated to remind us of the impermanency of life. *Higan* means the "other shore" which seems to be derived from the Sanskrit word, *Paramita*. It means "the state in which one has gone to the other shore after practicing the six virtues: namely, the exercise of giving, morality, patience, positive doing, penetration and perfect wisdom. The practice of these virtues is essential for all Buddhists to attain Buddhahood. The other shore symbolizes Nirvana in contrast to this shore, the mundane world of Samsara. It is the perfect annihilation of the repetitious cycle of life and death which we are treading. The Pure Land in which Amida Buddha is residing is on the other shore, while the abode of sentient beings is on this shore.

The celebration of *Higan* was started in Japan some 1200 years ago. According to historical records, in the 25th year of the Enryaku era (806 A.D.), the Japanese government ordered the priests of the Kokubunji temples, established by the government in every province throughout Japan, to recite the Diamond Sutra at this time of the season. This sutra shows the way of attaining the supreme wisdom which is as strong as a diamond. In the Heian and Kamakura periods, some 800 years ago, people were fond of listening to the recitation of *Kanmuryojukyo* at the time of Higan so that they could be freed from suffering and be born into the Pure Land. In this sutra, the merits of contemplating various symbols are referred to. One of them is the contemplation of the setting sun. It reads, "You should form a thought and sit rigidly facing toward the west and contemplate the setting sun intently. As you have thus seen the sun, let that image remain clear and fixed, whether your eyes be shut or open." They regarded it as the most important passage to be recited in those days, because at this time the sun sets exactly in the west.

During the Edo period, some 300 years ago, it was believed that for polishing mirrors the best day of the year was the *Chunichi*, or middle day of *Higan*, which would insure the brightness of minds and mirrors as well. At the Todaiji temple at Nara there is a special ceremony called *Omizutori*, the taking of purified water, which takes place just prior to the Higan season. On the night of March 11 and 12, purified water is taken from the sacred well and is poured on the image of the eleven-faced Kannon, the Bodhisattva Avalokitesvara. It signifies the cleansing of minds before facing the first sign of the new season. It is also at that time that branches of pine trees are burnt and these are waved above the heads of the people and are believed to cast out all evils from their hearts.

Such ceremonies in various forms are held in most Buddhist temples at this time of the year. They are of pure Japanese origin since nothing similar was known in India and China. The customs of visiting temples and grave-yards are common to all people throughout the country. People bring flowers, incense-sticks, water or food to be offered to the deceased, and meet them with fresh minds to report their well-being. During this period, the devout Buddhist begins his pilgrimage by visiting various temples. Such visitations were originally founded by Kobo Daishi (774–835 A.D.), founder of the Shingon Sect, on Shikoku island, where a large number of pilgrims can still be seen journeying from one temple to another. They are seen dressed in white and make the journey ringing handbells and chanting sacred verses in chorus. It is a charming and impressive scene in the peaceful villages of Japan.

∽ ∽ ∽

3. HANAMATSURI, THE BUDDHA'S BIRTHDAY

For the Christian, Christmas is the most joyous day, celebrating the birth of Jesus Christ; for the Buddhist, *Hanamatsuri* (Flower Festival) is the happiest day commemorating the birth of Gautama Buddha. On this day all Buddhists in China, Korea, Japan and the United States celebrate the Buddha's birthday at their respective places such as temples, churches, and parks with flower-covered shrines.

In India about 2500 years ago King Suddhodana

ruled the northern kingdom of Magadha. He had no children and he was anxious to have a son. After long expectation, his long cherished hope was fulfilled when the good news reached him that his wife, Queen Maya, had borne a son.

The Gautama Buddha was thus born at the Lumbini Garden when Queen Maya was on her way to her parent's home to give birth to her child. Legend tells us that when he was born, he took seven steps and pointed to heaven with his right hand and to the earth with his left hand, and proclaimed: "Here I am who is destined to be the most honorable one on this earth." This was a declaration of independence, independence from tradition, luxury and politics of this world. Although he was priviledged to take over his father's possessions, he did not wish to be possessed by them. He stood solely on his own feet, and came into this world as a unique human being who was not impressed by the conventional way of life and outer appearances.

It seems that the Buddha's birth took place in India on April 8, although the southern Buddhists celebrate it on the first full-moon day of May. Fa-hsien (399–414 A.D.) a renowned Chinese monk, mentioned in his travels that a fancy parade took place at Pataliputra in India on April 8 for the celebration of Buddha's birth. In China the first celebration of Buddha's birth is said to have taken place on April 8 in the later Chao Dynasty (319–353 A.D.), and in Japan it was first held in 606 A.D. at Gankoji Temple near Nara by the order of the Empress Suiko. On this day, the shrine, decorated with flowers, is put in the gathering place, and the statue of the Infant Buddha is enshrined in it. It symbolized the beautiful Lumbini Garden where the Buddha was born. It is sometimes carried on a white elephant in a parade suggesting that she brought the Buddha from heaven to the womb of his mother, Queen Maya. People gather around the shrine and pour sweet tea on top of the statue of the Infant Buddha as a substitute for the perfume which is said to have been poured by celestial beings. The ceremony is, therefore, called *"Kanbutsu-e"* (Tea-pouring ceremony on the Buddhá).

ᖇᖇᖇ

4. O-BON, THE BUDDHIST MEMORIAL DAY

The word *O-bon* is an abbreviation of ura-bon, the Sanskrit Ullambana which means literally "being hung upside down." It implies unbearable suffering which is felt, physically or spiritually, when one is hung upside down.

The legend tells us that in India there was a man called Maudagalyayana (Mokuren in Japanese). When he became one of the Buddha's disciples, he gained deep insight into the nature of existence. To his surprise he found his dead mother, thin and raw-boned, in the state of Ullambana, yearning for food and water. He immediately brought them to her, but she could not take them because, at the moment she was about to take them, they turned into fire. The astonished son hurried back to the Buddha to tell the whole story, and asked why she had to suffer. The Buddha quietly answered that it was inevitable because nobody took care of her before and after her death. Maudagalyayana felt sorry for the selfishness which he had shown before he became the Buddha's disciple. He was simply egocentric and took care of no one but himself.

When Maudagalyayana begged the Buddha for a way to rescue his mother, the Buddha advised him to summon all the monks nearby and hold a memorial service for her by offering food, clothing and other necessities to the monks and whole congregation. The Buddha further advised that July 15 is the best time to hold the service as all the monks come out from their summer retreat on this day, pure and free. The disciple was very much relieved by the Buddha's advice. He held the service as advised by the Buddha, and finally saved his mother from hunger and isolation in the other world.

Usually the *O-bon* services take place for four days beginning July 15. They are conducted by the ministers in front of a special altar made in the temple which is decorated with colorful lanterns and small paper banners in five colors. At the parishioners' homes, small altars are also made, and the spirits of their ancestors are believed to visit their old homes during this season. The first day of *O-bon* is called *Mukae-bon* or the welcoming day, and the last day, *Okuri-bon* the farewell day. On the eve of the *Mukae-bon* the parishioners go to the grave yard carrying beautiful lanterns and welcome the spirits of their ancestors back to their home. Horses and bullocks of cucumbers and egg-plants, with legs of dried grass stems, are prepared in front of the tombstone for them to mount. At home the parishioners enjoy a happy reunion with the spirits by holding a special feast with cake, fresh fruits and vegetables. During this season, the merry-go-round *Bon* dance is held in the church precincts in connection with the *Bon* service. It is said to please the invited spirits as well as the people attending. On the last day of *Okuri-bon*, the parishioners send off those spirits with a *Shoryobune*, a miniature boat, filled with all kinds of food, or with a lighted lantern. It is said that the boats will go across the ocean and reach the other shore safely so that until the next *O-bon* the spirits need never feel hungry nor lonesome in the other world.

∽ ∽ ∽

5. JODO-E, THE BUDDHA'S ENLIGHTENMENT DAY

The *Jodo-e* falls on December 8 on which day Gautama Siddhartha was fully enlightened under the Bodhi Tree at Budhagaya, and became the Buddha, the Supremely Awakened One.

After Gautama left his father's palace, he spent six long years in search of truth. He visited various ascetics and mystics who were detached from this world and exercised their austere disciplines. They taught him spiritual supremacy over materialism and vice versa by torturing their bodies to the point of attaining the highest state of mind where they became one with God. So, too, did Gautama, and yet in his pain and hunger he could

not gain anything but the miserable existence of his mind
and body. He wandered around and sought more intensely the best solution which could satisfy him and lead
him to deliverance from the fetter of this world. However, he failed to find any solution in the existing thoughts
and exercises.

When Gautama reached the River Nairanjana, he
found a good place in the forest for meditation. After he
sat down there, the darkness stole all around him, and he
was several times tempted by Mara, the master of sensual
pleasure, to give up his austere discipline. He struggled
and finally drove her away and fainted because of hunger and fatigue. When he awoke, he saw a country
girl, Sujata, passing by, and he accepted a bowl of curds
from her since he realized that a healthy mind could not
be gained in a body that was weak and ill. He went to
bathe in a nearby river, and sat under the Bodhi tree,
strengthened, refreshed, and relaxed. He deeply recognized at this moment that neither materialism (self indulgence) nor the extreme of spirituality (self torture) is
the way of deliverance from the fetters of this world; but
the Middle Way, the balancing and transcendence of
both materialism and spirituality is the way. He finally
found the way which was sound and healthy for his mind
and body at the age of 35.

As the morning star shone in the dawning light of the
east, Gautama attained enlightenment, the perfect
awareness of life, and he declared, "I am the supremely
awakened one." From that time on, he was born anew.
He came out of the forest full of confidence and convic-

tion, and began to preach that man must regulate his way of life according to Truth, and not according to tradition. He clearly showed the way to people who were suffering and tormented because of ignorance of the Reality of life.

Chapter 6

Explanation of Buddhist Symbolic Objects

THE BUDDHIST OBJECT OF WORSHIP

1. Buddha's Image

It is impossible to express Amida Buddha in physical form because he is nothing but the attributes of Wisdom and Compassion found in the supreme reality. However, we express these in the most ideal human form, namely, in the image of the historical person, Gautama Siddhartha, because he acquired such virtue when he attained enlightenment. In the case of the statue of Amida Buddha, he is usually depicted standing with an eye half closed, with his right hand raised making a circle with his index finger and thumb, and with his left hand palm upward stretched out toward the worshippers. The whole figure expresses complete inward harmony and peace and at the same time dynamic compassion to save all sentient beings.

2. The Main Altar in the Chancel

The statue of Amida Buddha is enshrined on the main altar, which is situated in the center of the chancel, since it is the main object of worship for all Jodo Buddhists. He is sometimes accompanied by his two attendants, *Seishi* and *Kannon,* the two attributes of Amida Buddha, namely, Wisdom and Compassion.

3. *The Second Altar*

The image of Zendo (Shan-tao in Chinese), the Chinese founder of Jodo Buddhism, is enshrined in the second altar, which is situated on the right hand side of the chancel. He is highly respected as the first interpreter of Buddhism in a popular form.

4. *The Third Altar*

The image of Honen, the Japanese founder of Jodo Buddhism, is enshrined in the second altar, which is situated on the left hand side of the chancel.

5. *Butsudan (Family Buddhist Altar)*

The *butsudan* is found in most Buddhist homes. It enshrines the image or picture of Amida Buddha, and is always kept clean and decorated with fresh flowers. Most people offer incense, rice, and water every morning and make *gassho* in the presence of Amida Buddha and the spirits of the deceased, vowing for things to be done better each day.

6. *I-hai (The Memorial Tablet)*

The Buddhist posthumous name of the deceased, given by the minister upon the passing-away of a person, is inscribed or written on the memorial tablet. The temporary *i-hai* is given either by the mortuary or the church, which is to be replaced by the permanent one after 49 days of mourning. The permanent *i-hai* is put in front of the Amida Buddha's image in the family altar.

7. *Kaimyo (Buddhist Posthumous Name)*

The *kaimyo* was first given to the monk or novice who went through the initiation ceremony and accepted the Buddhist precepts. Later it was also given to the layman who went through the initiation ceremony upon his death. The *kaimyo* of the deceased is written in Chinese characters denoting the virtue of his past deeds and is inscribed on the *i-hai* (memorial tablet) or on the tombstone.

8. *Juzu (Buddhist Rosary)*

The *juzu*, a long circle of beads joined together on a string, usually consists of 108 beads symbolizing our 108 worldly passions. It is said that when one vows to the Buddha for each bead on the string, his mind and body shall be freed from worldly passions. The largest bead in the middle represents the Buddha, the two beads on each side represent our parents or Wisdom and Compassion, and the rest represent each of us. The string represents a uniting force to strengthen our fellowship. The *juzu* should be carried all the time with reverence on the left wrist, and is grasped by the right hand.

9. *Candle*

The candle is used as an offering to the Buddha. It symbolizes the Wisdom and Compassion of Buddha which illuminates the darkness of ignorance and greed.

It also symbolizes those of us who wish to become the "candle-light in the dark."

10. The Gong

The gong is used to call attention to the beginning of the service. During the service it is used as punctuation. The striking sound of the gong reminds us of the awakening from our monotonous life and its diminishing sound the impermanence of life.

11. Incense

Incense, either in stick or powder form, is used as an offering to the Buddha, signifying the act of purifying our minds and bodies when we come to worship the Buddha. The smoke of incense burns away our impure minds and its fragrant scent purifies our minds. The offering is usually done three times in order for us to take refuge in the *Three Treasures* (Buddha, Dharma, and Samgha).

12. Flowers

Flowers are offered as an expression of our gratitude to the Buddha and are reminders of the impermanence of our lives since their beauty has elements of decay and death. In Buddhism, the white lotus is regarded as the finest among the flowers because it blooms with exquisite beauty and purity even in the mud.

13. Mokugyo

The *mokugyo* is the wooden gong generally used for

keeping rhythm in chanting sutras and in chanting the Nembutsu during the ceremony. Other musical instruments such as drums, bells, wooden clappers, cymbals, etc. are also used in Buddhist ceremonies.

14. Kesa (Buddhist Surplice) and Wagesa (Buddhist Stole)

The *kesa* is made of patches of small pieces of cloth stitched together and is worn by Buddhist ministers and priests over the robe. The *kesa* originally developed from the robes worn by the monks at the time of Gautama Buddha. In his time, robes were made of old discarded rags patched together to cover the monks' bodies, thus avoiding any attachment to clothing.

The *wagesa* is a narrow circular band of cloth worn by either a Buddhist minister or layman. It is the simplified form of the kesa.

15. Pagoda

They were originally built to contain the ashes of the Buddha, but later became depositories for sutras. They are constructed chiefly of wood, but sometimes of stone, metal, clay or tiles. There are two kinds of pagodas—*Toso-to* and *Taho-to*. The *Toso-to* are of 3, 5, 7, 9 or 13 stories, and the *Taho-to* of 2. Most temples in Japan have some kind of pagoda. The stone, clay, and tile pagodas are generally constructed as tombs for the deceased.

16. Toba (Wooden Tablet)

The *kaimyo* (Buddhist posthumous name) of a deceased person is written on the *toba* and is dedicated to the Buddha at memorial anniversary services.

17. Sutra (Scriptures)

These are the Buddhist cannonical texts containing dialogues or discourses of the Buddha. There are two versions of Buddhist sutras: one version is written in Pali (Sutta), and the other written in Sanskrit (Sutra). The scriptures used in the Jodo Mission services are written in classical Chinese, but read with Japanese pronunciation, and are translated from Sanskrit originals.

18. Buddhist Monasteries, Temples and Churches

Buddhist monasteries are places for practicing Buddhist precepts and disciplines, where Buddhist monks and nuns lead the simplest kind of life. Buddhist temples are places of worship where images of Buddha are enshrined, and priests in charge officiate at the ceremonies. Buddhist churches are consecrated for public worship and services, which are conducted by ministers or lay leaders.

19. The Dharmachakra (Wheel of the Law)

This is the Buddhist symbol in the form of a wheel. The circle denotes the completeness of the Buddha's teaching, which is always in motion. The eight spokes symbolize the Eight-fold Path and the rim, all encompassing Wisdom and Compassion. The axle is the bar of truth on which the wheel turns, and the hub represents the Oneness of Life.

20. *The Swastika*

In India, the *Swastika* is a symbol of good fortune and happiness. It symbolizes the origin, existence, and perpetuity of life, and its four L's stand for the Buddha's eternal Life, immeasurable Light, and boundless Love for which we must constantly Labor.

21. *The Buddhist Flag*

The Buddhist flag which is made of five colors—blue, yellow, red, white, and orange, has been in use in Srilanka since 1882. In 1950 at the first World Buddhist Conference held at Colombo, a resolution was passed to accept it as the International Buddhist Symbol. The five colors of the flag represented the aura of the Buddha's body which was seen on the day of his Enlightenment. Blue stands for devotion, yellow for intellect, red for love, white for purity and orange for energy.

လ လ လ

THE BUDDHIST FORM OF WORSHIP

1. *Offering of Incense, Flowers, Rice, Sweets, Candles, Water or Money*

Offering is an expression of our gratitude to the Buddha for being able to listen to his wonderful teaching. They are also an expression of our thanksgiving to the deceased who have done so many good things for us.

2. *Gassho*

In *Gassho,* we place our palms together to express our

reliance, thankfulness, and Oneness with the Buddha. The right hand symbolizes the Buddha and the left hand the human being. When they are placed together, we feel that the Buddha is in us and we are in the Buddha. This perfect unity of men and the Buddha is the significance of *Gassho*.

3. Meditation

There are various kinds of meditation in Buddhism. The most important one is the contemplation of the image of Buddha. The purpose of meditation is to control and purify our minds and to attain the highest spiritual insight and tranquility. The practice of meditation is also useful in enabling us to think and solve our problems realistically.

4. Chanting Sutras

Chanting the Buddhist sutras is very effective for understanding Buddhist teachings as well as for praising of the Buddha. Particularly when we chant them in unison, the feeling of unity with Buddha may be heightened.

5. Uttering the Nembutsu

The constant uttering of "Namu Amida Butsu" requires the full participation of our minds and bodies. Through this practice our minds and bodies are naturally directed to the Buddha, and this verbal expression results in the growth of spiritual and physical maturity.

6. Sitting in Meditation

When we sit in meditation, we should have an open mind and abandon all consciousness of body and mind. Next, we should not think about anything nor excite any feeling. Our minds should be like polished mirrors. Sit straight, and put the right foot on the left thigh, and then put the left foot on the right thigh. To inhale, breathe deeply through the nose. We gradually become one with the Buddha and enlightenment is expected to occur.

7. Singing and Dancing

The adoration of the Buddha is expressed in the form of singing and dancing. These exercises lead us actively into a religious feeling of solemnity and spiritual warmth. Besides the singing of gathas in unison, the *Go-eika* singing with tiny bells is widely known. The *Raisanmai* dancing is also presented at grand ceremonies in praise of the Buddha.

PART IV.

BUDDHISM IN ACTION

Chapter 1

Buddhist Sermons in 5 Minutes

In our daily lives we wish that everything would go well, we would getting along well with others and solve all problems whatever they might be without any objections or obstacles. However, in our actual life, we must painfully realize that things do not always go as well as we wish. Often, we have to cope with criticism, hardship, or difficulties when we undertake a definite project. It seems that encountering problems—desirable or undesirable—is inevitable from the day of our birth. Some skeptics might say, "Stick to our own work, and we are easily criticized by others. Always obey others, and we are carried away. Either way does not work out well. So we like to escape into day-dreaming." This kind of attitude does not actually solve the problem. These people, pretending that they are standing aloof, still have to encounter the problems of their daily lives. The following are some of the ways of solving my problems which I have had in my way of life. I hope they will be of some use for your understanding of life.

ဢ ဢ ဢ

1. FROM SELFISHNESS TO THE ONENESS OF LIFE

One day in my lecture on manners and morals to Japanese Language School children, I told the fable about two goats on one side of a deep ravine. The only bridge was a narrow log thrown across the chasm. Both goats wanted to cross first. As they pushed and shoved, both fell off the log and were dashed to pieces on the rocks below. "Now class," I asked, "which would you want to be in crossing the bridge, first or last?" All the children answered, "Last." All but one. He wanted to be first. I asked why. "Because if everybody was last, nobody would ever get across the log!" This answer made me think of something else.

We often find young people sitting comfortably in a commuting bus while the elderly people stand, people who drive their cars hurriedly and always try to get ahead of each other, people who spend money recklessly for their own sakes and not for others, and people who always exaggerate their misfortunes while paying no attention to others. Psychiatrist Madison Presnell once said, "As a nation we are becoming more sefish. We do not want to get involved with the troubles of others." There is a strong trend in the nation of people to take care of themselves and not worry about the others. Because of their egoism people are prone to be diverted, separated and finally alienated from their true selves and from others. Almost everyday bloody strife is begotten

among the people in South Vietnam, Ireland, and
Middle East. All are struggling for their benefits.
Why should they fight and kill each other? Why should
they be divided among themselves? Is it inevitable that
people must fight and die because of the struggle for
existence? I do not think so. There must be some common denominator where they can meet each other without strife. We call this common denominator the Oneness
of Life.

そ そ そ

2. THE MIDDLE WAY OF LIFE

French philosopher, Blaise Pascal once said that we
have a two fold nature: namely greatness and wretchedness. In this "*Pensees*" Pascal said that it is dangerous to
make man see too clearly his equality with the brutes
without showing him his greatness. It is also dangerous
to make him see his greatness too clearly, apart from his
vileness. It is still more dangerous to leave him in ignorance of both. But it is very advantageous to show him
both. Man must not think that he is on a level either with
the brutes or with the angels, nor must he be ignorant of
both sides of his nature; but he must know both. According to Pascal, man in nature is a mean between everything and nothing. Likewise, the Buddha taught the
Middle Way avoiding both extremes of indulgence and
aloofness. First, there is the extreme of indulgence to the
desires of the body, the whims of the mind and the pride
of life, that comes naturally to one who cherishes the

notion that this world is a real world and this life an end in itself. Second, there is the opposite extreme that comes naturally to one who cherishes the notion that a world of truth is the only reality; to one it comes easy to renounce this world and to go to an extreme of ascetic discipline and to tortue one's body and mind unreasonably. The Buddha taught the Middle Way that lies between these two extremes. He gave us a parable which goes on like this. Suppose a log is floating in a river. If the log docs not become grounded, or does not sink, or is not taken out by a man, or does not decay, ultimately it will reach the sea. Life is like this log caught in the current of a great river. If a person does not become attached to a life of self-indulgence, or, by renouncing life, becomes attached to a life of self-torture; if a person does not become proud of his virtue or of his evil acts; if in his search for Enlightenment he does not become contemptuous of delusion or fear it; such a person is following the Middle Way. If we become attached to things, just at that moment, all at once, the life of delusion begins. The one who follows the Middle Way will not cherish regrets, neither will he cherish fear or anticipations, but, with equitable and peaceful mind, will meet whatever comes to him. Therefore, the Infant Buddha stood solely on his own feet and pointed to heaven with his right hand and to the earth with his left hand, proclaiming the uniqueness of the human being who should balance the sacred and profane and follow the Middle Way of Life.

3. THE IMPORTANCE OF ORIGINAL ENTHUSIASM

Nothing is more difficult to evaluate than the growth of our skills in the light of our age and the number of years we have engaged in any work. In as much as we lack concentrated effort to accomplish our undertakings when we are young, it is a natural tendency to proceed with pure and intense zeal. However, when we attain some degree of maturity by accumulating experience and fulfilling our original objectives—there is a tendency to proceed not with the vigor and dedication of youth but to plod along indifferently with the minimum of effort necessary to reach further heights.

We have an intense desire to accomplish something by ourselves, but some failures are inevitably attached to our undertakings. In the course of experience, such failures occur less frequently. We owe much of our progress to our failures. This progress begins when our mistakes lead us to react. And I wonder: Does it not do us good if we put our original enthusiasm into our routine responsibilities?

In the book called *Kakyo*, written by the Japanese Noh dance master, Zeami, there appeared a phrase which stressed the necessity of retaining the original eagerness and caution.

Day by day, year by year, nothing seems to change in our daily lives, but we must set aside definite periods of time for self-evaluation in this continuous passage of time in order to renew our strength of purpose. New Year's Day, then, can be made a starting point for this effort. I believe that the idea of retaining our original enthusiasm could be a wholesome reminder to renew critically our daily activities.

 captions ∾ ∾ ∾

4. SUFFERING IS BLISS

Psychologists say that there is a point of no return when we are reaching or going beyond our limit in doing things. Some people who have been too patient or who have endured beyond their capacity, will lose competence. When the pressures become too great in business or professions, people can lose their ability to make decisions. Therefore, when we feel we need relaxation or complain about our work, it is a signal to tell us that we are overworked. Psychologists suggest that when we are worried or become tired, "We should not worry as it must be tough," and should say, "beyond this point you are exhausted, so stop doing things." However, who can tell exactly when we can proceed or stop? Maybe the decision must be made by ourselves. Then, we must always find the time and place to take a rest when exhausted. But such exhaustion is easily felt because of our weak nature. When we meet pressure, there are three ways of reacting to it. The first is to submit to it by giving up our work. The second is to endure or change our pace and tactics in order to accomplish our task. And the third is to positively attack and bring it under our control. Only in this third way do we require a strong will and positive thinking, so that we can extend our limits in doing things to the furthest extent.

∾ ∾ ∾

5. THE IMPORTANCE OF ALWAYS SMILING

One day my teacher told me that he believed that men become sad by crying. This theory was established by William James. I had never heard such an absurd theory before. I thought no one could cry without feeling sad, and there was no man in the world so foolish that he could show anger without being emotionally upset. My teacher, however, told me that he had had an interesting experience while he was in China.

In China it is the custom to invite many priests when someone dies and also they take great pride in inviting so-called beldames, whose business is to cry all the way to the cemetery. Of course, they have no reason for crying other than for the purpose of obtaining money. My teacher observed that these beldames were crying from the bottom of their hearts after finishing their business. This phenomenon: "When one cries one becomes sad" is described as "consciousness stimulated by bodily action" by William James.

When I reflected upon this, one idea came to my mind. If we smile happily, can we not become lighthearted? After considering these thoughts, I became convinced that a smiling face could make us happy and pleasant.

6. WE SHOULD BE REACHABLE

Nothing is more awful than an encounter with an unreachable person. No matter how much we persuade him with sincerity and humility, he does not want to understand what we are trying to say. We do not ask his consent nor do we blame his ignorance. What we want is his attention and understanding of our standpoint. We like to talk things over which are pertinent to both of us and see what the results will be. If he cannot lend his ear to what we are saying, we should listen to his standpoint in turn, and exchange views frankly until we reach a complete understanding of each other. However, if he cannot or is unwilling to do so, what should we do? Of course it is not our business to deal with him persistently, as it is often said, "Do not persist with the people who want to escape from us," but if he causes trouble for us, we just cannot look at him vacantly. Such a person often does something unthinkable. He himself is very much confused, therefore, he can confuse others even when nothing happens. Even though he may cause trouble for others, he does not care and is often pleased to do so.

Such a person laughs at others so much that they worry about him. Such a person can commit suicide without difficulty and might easily kill others. It is extremely difficult to deal with such an unreachable person. We find such a person among stubborn men or hysterical women. Let us not become such unreachable people, but be sensible men.

7. THE IMPORTANCE OF OPEN-MINDEDNESS

The present world-wide competition of nuclear ex-
periments and space flights seems to keep each nation
busy in its efforts to exceed other nations. The competition of such scientific research is sometimes favorable for
the advancement of civilization, but is sometimes unfavorable because it destroys human lives. The more each
nation secretly attempts to compete with another in
research, the more misunderstanding and overspecula-
tion are bound to come between them. Under-developed
nations tend to keep their research secret, although they
usually copy procedures from more advanced nations.
Likewise, inferior people tend to hide their efforts and
work secretly in order to astonish others when the secrets
are revealed. This is very unfair. Fair play is an utmost
necessity for nations and people alike in order to avoid
unnecessary friction among themselves, and research
should be utilized by any or all nations for the common
good and welfare of all people.

∾ ∾ ∾

8. STUDY THE PAST DISCOVERIES

Once a renowned English poet, Edmund Blunden,
pointed out the fact that all of the discoveries and inven-
tions made by the scholars and scientists of the present
world might have been found by people in the past, but
who were unaware of their significance.

Let us take an example in the history of the synecology

of honey bees. "For Samson the powerful, a lion seemed nothing but a trifle, and he killed a lion when it came into his sight. After a few days, he went to see the dead lion with his lover, and then he realized that beautiful bees were flying about it." This is a passage taken from the Old Testament (Judges 14:5-9). Actually they were not bees but flies. It was not until the middle of the 17th century that a scientist found the answer and described the phenomenon of honey bees accurately.

However, long before a scientist did find the phenomenon of honey bees, there was a man who accurately described it. Vergilius, one of the greatest poets of the Roman Empire, wrote about them in his "*Georgia*" the ecology of honey bees. Until recently nobody knew that a poet of ancient Rome discovered honey bees.

∾ ∾ ∾

9. THE REQUIREMENTS OF LEADERSHIP

In any organization, school, office, club or otherwise, an able leader needs to have at least three important qualities in order to govern his fellow men.

First, the leader should have an understanding of his fellow men. If he expects his fellow men to work effectively, he must understand their feelings and try to make their working place as pleasant and friendly as possible. In order to do this, the leader must be able to recognize the capabilities of each individual and make assignments accordingly. And then, once he assigns his fellow men to their right places, he should trust their work to the fullest extent.

The second quality is that the leader should be competent and reflect this competence in relations with his fellow men. In the past, the leader controlled his fellow men by means of forceful orders or by affable remarks, but nowadays these no longer are effective. The leader cannot be respected if he is not competent; without their respect he cannot be in command of his fellow men.

The third quality is that the leader should make clear to his fellow men the meaning and purpose of his organization and its activities. No matter how fine an ideal he imposes upon his fellow men, unless they thoroughly understand it, few will work to their utmost. The leader should always know the direction of his work. In order to achieve this he must be ready to guide his fellow men toward it.

If the leader does not have all of these three qualities, he should resign his post promptly, and be replaced by a more able leader. By doing so, it will be more profitable to him, to his fellow men and to his organization.

∾ ∾ ∾

10. WHEN WE ARE ABUSED

There is a story which was prevalent among the children in old-time Japan. It goes like this. Once upon a time there were two frogs traveling from two big cities—Tokyo and Kyoto—who happened to meet each other at the foot of Mt. Fuji. Each was boasting that his own city was larger than the other's and defamed the other city as smaller and dirtier. There was no end to the argument, so they finally made a decision to climb the mountain to see another city so that they might compare their own cities with it. After a long struggle of climbing, they finally reached the top of the mountain and stood up on their two tiny legs, looking down the other side to see the city. They looked at each other and said, "Now, you see that my city is larger than yours! Your city is much smaller and dirtier than mine!" However, the city they saw did not seem to be larger than their own cities. Why? Because their eyes were on the back of their heads! Only the sun was smilingly gazing down on them.

We have seen so many people around us who, like these frogs, boast about themselves and at the same time abuse, blame or find fault with others. This seems to be a common practice of the people in this world. However, imagine those who become the focus of such condemnations. They cannot have a good feeling when they hear about them. They also like to take revenge on others in some way or another. Here lies the never ending series of conflict among ourselves.

Then, what should we do when we are involved in such a situation accidentally or otherwise? Buddhism gives us a good story which leads us to a solution. It is the story of a man who lived in India a long time ago. He was always jealous of everyone he met, and nobody liked him. One day when he met Gautama Buddha he also became jealous of his fame and openly attacked him verbally. No matter how much this man made nasty remarks about him, the Buddha kept silent and patiently listened to what he wanted to say. When the man became exhausted from speaking ill of him, the Buddha quietly said, "My dear son, supposing a man presented his gift to another, and yet if he did not receive it, to whom does that gift belong?" The man bluntly answered, "Of course, the gift belongs to the owner." "That's right," the Buddha said, "And you abused me, and yet I didn't receive it. To whom does this accusation belong?" The man could not answer immediately. After a moment, he realized his foolishness and promised the Buddha that he would never abuse others.

Of course, criticisms after fair judgements and with no derogatory connotations should be promoted as much as possible in order to make us much better people, but we must keep in mind that those who like to abuse, blame or find fault with others are like the ones who spit into the sky. They cannot stain the sky but only make themselves filthy.

∽ ∽ ∽

11. WHEN WE FACE ANXIETY

Have you ever experienced a feeling of being submerged in a desperate state of mind? Anyone who falls into such a state of mind can hardly revive his cheerful feeling. We may experience this in our daily lives. Psychologists define it as a "slump" which is mainly caused by our emotional, mental or physical condition. When one is "in a good mood," he finds pleasure in doing things and is able to overcome seemingly insurmountable obstacles in his daily life. However, once he enters into a "slump," he is apt to find little good in any situation and show his cheerlessness to others.

We can easily identify one who is in a slump and is not in his usual cheerful mood from the following: He (1) seems to become quiet and moody; (2) argues and quarrels with others; (3) shows his temper or blames others; (4) throws things or even destroy things; (5) gets sarcastic; (6) cries, slam doors or drawers; (7) shouts or screams; (8) releases his anger on other members of the family or on pets; (9) sulks and acts rudely toward others; (10) smokes or drinks excessively; (11) overeats and drives recklessly. These aggravate his bad mood, and nothing good can be gained from this misbehavior.

Cheerlessness arises from problems. We display unpleasant feelings when we have realized that we are unable to solve problems as we meet them. Therefore, in the first place, we must find out what is the real cause of the problem which is making us depressed, and directly attack it boldly. It is said in an old proverb. "Touch a thistle timidly, and it pricks you; grasp it boldly, and its spines crumble." Nothing good results as long as we do not act on our unsolved problems. We can often overcome the difficulty by directly attacking the problem we meet.

Direct attack is, of course, the best way to meet our problems; nevertheless, we need to be realistic in evaluating the situations that we face. It may be that we need

The front picture shows the image of guardian king enshrined at Kohukuji Temple in Nara.

to change our tactic or our goals. When we encounter a road block on a trip, the well-marked detour is provided in order to proceed further. Although with many of our problems no well-marked detour is provided, we need to compensate by adopting a substitute activity to achieve the desired end. Compensation restores our confidence and courage and helps to overcome feelings of inferiority which may have resulted from failure in the pursuit of our goal. Therefore, I believe that the best policy for this situation is to do whatever we want to, and to direct our unpleasant feelings in a better and more constructive direction. We should engage in sports and games, take a walk, study, talk things over with good listeners, play music or sing or listen to music, watch TV or go to a movie or read books, or perform chores for others. The above seem to compensate for our unpleasant state of mind.

If we can not find anything to do, the last chance to restore our confidence and courage is to practice the calling of the Nembutsu, the constant repetition of "Namu Amida Butsu." It contains no magical power but will almost miraculously restore our will power. Because the practice of the Nembutsu requires our emotional, mental and physical participation in order to achieve our absolute goal, and—the total realization of ourselves is identified with the ideal Self. It is a very simple and easy practice for those who have nothing else to do. Some people who find themselves unable to cope with problems usually react by simply giving up and withdrawing from situations or attempting to escape through day-dreaming. They no longer face their problems and will gradually be alienated from them. This is called regression. It usually means reverting to a less mature form of behavior and is a dangerous sign of the disintegration of personality.

In order to achieve a well-integrated personality, we need to look at ourselves realistically. Are we pursuing a desirable course of action in meeting problems? If we are compensating, is it a type of compensation which is constructive? Are we using too many crutches for our failures? It is absolutely necessary to choose these ways: direct attack, compensation, or calling the Nembutsu, and to adjust ourselves to the situations we face whenever they exist and wherever we are faced with them.

∾ ∾ ∾

12. DO WE MAKE THINGS ALIVE?

It might be a foolish thing to ask a question as "Do we make things alive?" because everything that exists on this earth is living without the aid of human power. Biologically, every living organism exists by its own power; no human power is required to make them live. However, there are certain things that exist which cannot be included in the above category: daily conversations, money, and our bodies.

Let us take our daily conversation. We hear many unpleasant words from those who consciously or unknowingly speak ill of others. Those who are showered with phrases such as, "Damn you" or "Shut up" naturally are embarassed, yet we hear these repeated frequently. These words not only embarrass others but quite frequently the speaker himself feels uncomfortable. Instead of using these words, words of gratitude and courtesy will no doubt please those who hear them. Some might say it is better to be criticized frankly rather then to receive empty compliments, but this becomes an exception. We can therefore divide words into two areas: living words and dead words. If we can minimize or e-radicate the dead words that displease others, we can make alive our daily conversations and promote friend-ship.

Of money, there are also two categories—living money and dead money. If we hoard, or spend money recklessly, money becomes dead. Instead of reckless spending, if we use it in a productive way, it becomes alive. The mere act of depositing money in a bank is a way in which money becomes useful. It enables bankers and investors to make money live, and, at the same time, the money yields financial returns in time. Thus, a large number of people benefit from this money, if we make use of it.

Our bodies are no different. We should not remain idle, for life on earth is short. Living in idleness may seem to be all right, but the more important thing is to use our bodies usefully and meaningfully. Working by ourselves will make others work, and then, we can taste the fruits of true pleasure from working cooperatively. Then we shall be able to promote good work and friendship without thinking about trifles, and our bodies shall become more healthy. Work, therefore, really serves a triple purpose.

I have heard it stated often that the power of water symbolizes the activity of human beings. That is, water moves by itself, and, at the same time, moves other objects; water never ceases to go its own way; water multiplies its force a hundred fold when it encounters obstacles; water cleans; and water fills the oceans. Water becomes a cloud when it evaporates; it becomes a mist when about to be changed into rain and snow; it becomes ice when frozen. Water never changes. Water creates when it takes action. Man and the tools of mankind, like the power of water, can create new things when used. Therefore, I firmly believe that mere possession of an article shall no longer determine its worth; its value becomes known only after putting it to use.

ᘓ ᘓ ᘓ

13. FROM TALKING TO DOING

One time, the noted American architect Philip Cortelyou Johnson said in an interview in *Vogue*: "I am sick and tired of all the word-minded people in this world. The word-minded people are the ones who set the standards. An artist or an architect conceives and creates; but then in the final analysis he's at the mercy of some writer—a man who uses up hours and days of his time asking him childish, idiotic, asinine questions and then, in a final irony, assesses him for all time. Why I'm submitting to it I don't know."

In like manner, I am tired of people who only sit back and bluntly abuse others by saying, "He is silly" or "You are wrong" without giving any sufficient reason for it. Also, I am tired of people who praise themselves by saying, "I am doing good" or "I am working hard." Whenever I hear them, I think these statements are false. The good man is good even though he *does not* state that "I am good." Others only recognize him as good or bad and diligent or idle through his total behavior and conduct.

These ego-centric people are mostly seeking their own benefit at the expense or sacrifice of others. Therefore, these narrow and closed-minded people are stagnant when anyone expresses ideas or opinions contrary to or different from theirs, and they live only in the dim-cell of their own darkened world. They do not progress because they have neither eyes to see things as they really are nor ears to listen to something which is better than what they possess. Their judgement is so quick and sharp that they do not give others a chance to express their own ideas and opinions nor do they agree with anyone who promotes new or better projects for the enrichment of us all. On the contrary, these individuals mostly favor or protect the certain kinds of people who simply follow or agree with them. When they realize that people are not in accord with them or that there are better things found in others, they get angry and begin to abuse them; or sometimes, because of jealousy, they spread erroneous news or plan secretly to make trouble for others. They are simply afraid of facing reality directly and try to protect their confined and dead ego and to cover their own inferiority and fault by attacking others.

I believe that it is not good to relegate people to two different camps, good or bad and right or wrong. If one does so, never-ending mischiefs and conflict are bound to multiply among them. Prince Regent Shotoku, the great advocate of Buddhism in 6th Century Japan, wrote a constitution and in it he said, "Do not become angry just because someone opposes your ideas or opinions. Everyone has a mind and every mind comes to a decision and the decisions will not always be alike. If he is right, you are wrong; if you are right, he is wrong; you are not a genius nor is he an idiot. Both disputants are men of ordinary minds. If both are wise men or both foolish men, their argument is probably an endless circle. For this reason, if your opponent grows angry you should give more heed to yourself lest you too are in error. One can seldom attain all he wishes. Therefore, have a complete understanding of the reality you face and view others with tolerance." Likewise, we must open our eyes and lend our ears to everyone and respect others' points of view. We must also understand the limitations of our capacity and conduct ourselves with humility. Broad, open-minded and modest behavior certainly bridges the gaps between us and enables all of us to promote virtue and become much better people in a much better society. Therefore, before we complain, grumble or judge others, or after we are abused by others, the only way we can show and prove our superiority is to do what we can with what we have where we are now, even though no one appreciates or sees us.

In Buddhism, people are important, Buddhism, of course, is an idea. But nothing happens to an idea until it takes possession of somebody. After that, what happens to it depends upon what kind of people are working on it; upon their intelligence, their persistence, and their devotion. It depends upon how clearly and completely an individual can understand a situation and see how he is related to it; and then upon his willingness to translate his perceptions into action. Therefore, only in this action can we be better off and show to the world what we really are and what we will be, without looking for our neighbors' opinions and without looking back on our fixed selves.

∾ ∾ ∾

14. WHAT IS REAL PLEASURE?

Of all the needs characterizing the human race, none appears more pervasive than the seeking of pleasure in this tormenting world. In any age, needless to say, pleasure has been sought by all men to temporarily divert them from their world. In modern times such a desire manifests itself in many ways: drinking of wine, smoking of cigarettes, an addiction to sports and daily recreation by way of the radio and TV set, or the habitual attendance of movie theaters. We cannot live a day without indulging in some form of pleasure.

This abundance of pleasure never ceases; it has an insidious ability to expand to the point of enveloping and destroying everything else. This is a nationwide trend which we can do very little to negate except to gaze upon it with objectivity and calm judgment. Possibly, one thing that could be done is to channel this tide of pleasure-seeking into a more constructive direction.

Perhaps it would be helpful at this time to consider two points of view which I feel characterize "Pleasure."

First, pleasure is a state of mind which we achieve with expanded effort. For example, reading books, conquering seemingly insurmountable mountains, or even leaping over a new height in the polevault constitutes this sort of pleasure. It requires some effort, at times hardship, to attain the goal or fulfil the purposes set forth by ourselves. In short it is the satisfaction gained by setting goals, and through endurance, actively overcoming the physical and psychological obstacles in the path of achievement. This variety of pleasure is comparable to the drinking of cold water after having reached a fountain with thirst. The second variety of pleasure is a passive one which can be captured without taxing our physical or mental energy. Seeing a movie, drinking wine, and smoking cigarettes—all these serve to satisfy our feelings and offers very little challenge. Thus, it is a passive pleasure for which we need not put forth any effort or endure any hardship since the means are conveniently provided.

The former can be said to be "mental pleasure," and the latter, "sensual pleasure." As we examine the modern trend of pleasure, we can hardly ignore the fact that most people—young and old—are actively seeking the latter, sensual pleasure. We are apt to stake our lives on immediate pleasure due to the aleatory nature of our personalities. Everything is lost by skipping the process of doing things in order to attain an immediate goal. For example, we seek this type of pleasure in gambling, sex, and rock and roll music in which the chief aim is to satisfy our suddun impulses.

This situation exists, because of the uneasiness of life which vexes our civilization, a civilization of which no man dares to forecast its future. After the war, an atmosphere of instability such as the fluctuation of prices, financial panics, and moral decadence has haunted this world. Mankind has been forced to seek immediate pleasure, even though meaningless, to help forget this undesirable phenomenon. The epicurean or nihilistic flavor of life has so permeated our thought that escape is impossible; thus, increasing excitement and thrills are required in our modern life to escape our troublesome and shortsighted world. A constant barrage of noise and motion from radios, TV's, cars, and so forth is utilized to relieve us. One can easily imagine the situation which will follow if this phenomenon is suddenly jerked to a stop. No doubt, a strange and tearing stillness and vacantness will occupy our minds only to further remind us of the uncertainty of life.

♆ ♆ ♆

15. THE PROBLEM OF DEATH

Someone aptly said that the real pleasure in life is found in expectation. Likewise, we can say that the real fear of death is also found in its expectation. As long as there is life, there is death. It is an inevitable and inescapable reality which we have to encounter sooner or later. The problem of death has been discussed by many people in the past, and yet nobody seems to have given us an adequate answer to this question. It is the most essential and also most difficult question to discuss because nobody has as yet experienced death, and been able to discuss it.

Usually people have understood death as the most dreadful and awful experience, and in order to escape from it they wish to be born into Heaven thereafter. They literally believe that there exists a Heaven and Hell in another world. Artists have encouraged this idea by depicting vividly the joyous scene of Heaven and the horrible sight of Hell. People yearn for the presence of a savior who will carry them to Heaven, and the religious in turn demand them to believe in his saving power.

However, some people in the contemporary age gradually have lost interest in the problem of death. Although they cannot deny the impact of death, they simply avoid discussion of death because it is a hateful event and the destruction of their happy lives. And when they realize that death is an inescapable and a concrete reality for them, they begin to fuss and cannot do anything but be stupified. Some of them become absent-minded and lose courage and confidence in life. Others try to forget the dreadfulness of death by drinking alcoholic beverages excessively or by devoting all their time to their work. However, they painfully realize that they gain nothing and ever more intensify their desire to live. Then, what should they do? Some of them return to the traditional way of believing in the existence of a savior who will lead them to Heaven; others stand boldly or timidly on the edge of life and death without any idea of being born into the other world. Whoever they may be, they react against death in their own way and at the final moment they quickly pass away just like going to sleep.

A few years ago, Professor Hideo Kishimoto of Tokyo University underwent a medical examination and was told by his doctor that he was already very sick with cancer. He was shocked to hear this bad news for the first time, and moreover, he was told that he would live only for a half a year. From this time on, he began to think about death quite seriously, and evenmore intensified his desire to live. He suffered and struggled to escape from this hateful reality. However, knowing that escape was impossible, he began to work more furiously than before. He was willing to try anything which might distract him in order to use up all his energy. He would fall asleep soundly at night. Despite his devotion to his work, he confessed that the more he devoted himself to a busy life the more he could not forget the dreadfulness of death. Finally he decided that death is a kind of farewell just like saying goodbye to one's parents when one leaves home every day. If one prepares for this parting in advance, one might somehow manage to face this reality and overcome it without fear. He thought, therefore, that death is nothing special; it is the continuation of one's repeated farewells in daily life. Thereafter, even though he was threatened by death, he managed to prolong his life for another eight years. Later on, he was completely at ease with death and each moment was for him so precious and meaningful that he could live well until his final moment. He was even thankful for the invasion of cancer, because without it he could never have discovered the meaning of life and death. Finally, on January 25, 1964, he took his last breath on his death bed, after saying goodbye to his family and his colleagues.

Professor Kishimoto's idea is very much like that of Dogen, the founder of Soto Zen Buddhism in Japan. He said, "Without thinking about your mind and body, you should simply throw yourself to the Buddha, then he will take care of you. If you simply follow him, you will become one with Buddha without worrying about yourself and will naturally refrain from thoughts of life and death." It is the state of mind where there is neither ego nor clinging to ego. Just let it work by itself without struggling. If we can attain this state of mind, death will be no more a fearful thing. Only serenity and peace will remain in us. Once we master death, nothing can be feared because death itself is the most fearful thing. We are able to anticipate death at any moment and to discharge our duties and work to the fullest extent. Nothing can be comparable to this joy in our lives. Therefore, wherever we are, we must "work as if we were to live forever, and live as if we were to die tomorrow."

∾ ∾ ∾

16. HOW TO BECOME A TRUE BUDDHIST

It seems to be an inescapable trend that a man is evaluated according to his "rank," "influence" or "wealth." Those who have these elements appear to enjoy their lives, but those who have not are obliged to make their living by reluctantly obeying the will of the more fortunate people. I believe nothing good comes from this situation, because there exists a sense of arrogance, pride and aggression on the side of the "have" people, and a sense of fear, obedience, and an inferiority complex on the side of the "have-not" people. I believe that the equality of human rights should be emphasized more intensely, so that any oppressive measures will be minimized or even eliminated. Moreover, contempt for unfortunate fellow beings should be avoided. The more powerful man is the one who should display more modesty. Therefore, there should be no distinction between rich and poor, nor should there be any prejudice between the "have" and "have not" people. Mutual understanding and cooperation will be gained if we firmly maintain this belief and practice it in our daily lives.

Once we become free from such discriminative measures, we must stand on the same footing and seek the truth inwardly as well as show kindness toward others. We must look at ourselves and our problems objectively and assume responsibility for our behavior and its consequences. We must take a problem-solving approach to life's questions without escaping from this suffering world. We must recognize our feelings and be able to express them with discretion. We must express our emotions in wholesome, constructive ways. We must assume heavy emotional burdens without "cracking-up" We must show evidence of social growth and must accept others for what they are. We must emancipate ourselves from childhood dependencies, and meet strangers easily without any embarrassment. We must accept and adjust to the rules and laws of the group of which we are a part and must make a constructive contribution to the world around us.

Also, we must have a sense of knowing where we are going—conscious or unconscious goals toward which we are striving; have few inner conflicts; live primarily for long-term values, rather than taking what we want at the moment. We must not show fear or anger regarding non essentials; if an emergency arises—whether it be a problem on the job, the loss of a loved one, or a war—we should not be upset for long, but face it with poise and hope, continuing in the same direction toward our goal. We must show social-mindedness and concern for the welfare of others, rather than a self-interest. We cannot be perfect in many of these things, but we should try to show growth step by step and from day to day.

A good-natured man might want to satisfy his feelings by becoming a "good man," but the more he devotes himself to this purpose, the more painfully he realizes that he does not deserve to be so called. (if he does, he is a fool or a hypocrite). Therefore, instead of becoming good men, we must strive to live *well* in our short span of life. I believe those who are sincerely attempting to do so, and yet are still unsatisfied, deserve to be called men of wisdom and compassion and at the same time true Buddhists.

∾ ∾ ∾

17. WHY I BECOME A BUDDHIST

Whenever I am asked by people, "Why did you become a Buddhist?" I simply answer, "Because I like Buddhism." However, this sort of answer does not seem to satisfy the curiosity of inquirers. Therefore, I would like to explain my motives and reasons, and at the same time to reevaluate my religion as a source of continuous inspiration and guiding light.

By some, Buddhism has been regarded as a heretic religion which was brought by immigrants from the Orient. Some others underestimate its value and say that it is an outdated religion which has in its character feudalistic, magical and mystical elements. Still others simply disregard Buddhism as something heterogeneous and show indifference to it. These viewpoints are quite understandable and there is no reason to resent them. Then, why have I chosen such a religion despite these unfavorable viewpoints? There are three basic reasons which can be singled out for my commitment to Buddhism.

In the first place, I was born into a Buddhist family. My parents are Buddhists who have long been ministering to people at their temple in Japan. From my childhood, I have been oriented and disciplined within the strong environment of Buddhist tradition, and its influence upon me is immeasurable.

In the second place, I was born a Japanese. This fact is of vital importance for my commitment to Buddhism. Buddhism is regarded as the representative religion of the Japanese. The highly refined forms of Japanese culture, as found in flower-arrangement, tea-ceremony, Haiku-poems, calligraphy, painting, judo, karate, archery, etc., are said to have been molded by the strong influence of Buddhism. However, Buddhism is often misunderstood or totally neglected by the Japanese themselves as well as foreigners. As a Japanese, I strongly felt that something should be done in order to make Buddhism known to the world in its true form. This urge naturally directed me to the study of Buddhism when I entered a Japanese college, and since then it has been my chief concern and subject of study.

In the third place, the more I learned of Buddhism the more I felt convinced that this was the religion I could confidently trust and rely upon, because it has no traffic with the artificial notions of correctness or superiority. It is descriptive and not prescriptive about our life problems: it only shows us how to find the beauty and the Oneness of all life which I mentioned elsewhere. Buddhism is, therefore, practical and is always related to us, our problems, our nature, and the dynamics of our development. This I could not possibly find in any other religion.

However, the three reasons mentioned above should be clarified further so that misunderstandings can be avoided. First of all, I do not like to be called a Buddhist in a nominal sense. There are many nominal Buddhists who call themselves "Buddhists." simply because they are born into Buddhist families or are members of Buddhist churches where they attend services occasionally. These nominal Buddhists, as someone said, are like those who write checks when they have no money in the bank. Unless we have money in the bank, we are frauds when we write check for $10,000. Likewise, we may call ourselves Buddhists, but unless our words and deeds correspond to that title, we are frauds. However, this does not mean that we can become perfect when we become Buddhists. My commitment to Buddhism does not mean that I am already a Buddhist but that I am becoming a Buddhist. Even though I may have faults and make mistakes in life, I commit myself to Buddhism in order to live better, strongly, meaningfully, and purposefully.

Secondly, I do not like to be called a Buddhist simply because I was born a Japanese. Buddhism is not a monopoly of the Japanese nor is it confined to the citadel of Japanese culture. It is a world religion, and its value can be appreciated by people regardless of race, nationality, color, or sex. If we find something to be best in Buddhism, which is lacking in other religions, why not introduce it to the world at large? Like the Caucasians who introduced their heritage from Europe, we should introduce our heritage from the Orient. If we lose our own heritage and bury our unique system of thought under the Western shadow, how can we contribute our share to the world?

Thirdly, I do not like to be called a fanatic Buddhist. A fanatic claims that only his religion possesses the Truth and that all other religions are false or at least incomplete. He takes it for granted that his religion is bound to win the allegiance of the whole human race, and will never stop until the rest of the people are converted into his fold. However, if all of us become the same type of person, think alike and behave alike, how can we enjoy the freedom of individuality and share the uniqueness of personality? Each religion is a unique system of thought in its own right and is the product of human need in its historical and cultural settings. Therefore, the diversity of doctrinal implications and experiential content of each religion must be highly respected. Although the unification of rules and modes of living are a modern trend which we are prone to follow, this does not mean that we must blindly agree to one creed or dogma. We have a right to our own beliefs too.

Because of these reasons, I chose Buddhism as my religion and my way of life, and I am very proud to be a Buddhist in addition to the fact that I was born a Japanese of a Buddhist family. Even though there are many respectable religions around me, I chose Buddhism because in it I find the solution to my life problems and the meaning of all life. I believe such a teaching is healthy and sound, and is helpful for the development of my potentiality and capacity. Therefore, I trust and rely upon Buddhism as my continuous inspiration and guiding light.

∾ ∾ ∾

18. THE TASK OF JAPANESE BUDDHISTS

The renowned American economist, Dr. Peter Drucker, is reported to have sent an inquiry to his Japanese friend, saying "There seems nothing noteworthy in the techniques and management of Japanese economy, but I wonder why it all of a sudden has become so prosperous. Let me know the secret." To him who visited Japan and taught the importance of business administration to his Japanese counterparts, the rapid development of Japanese economy seemed a miracle. It is true that it has expanded rapidly as supply and demand multiplied year by year.

How about the political and religious situations in Japan? The backstage politics and seemingly premodern religious traditions which still prevail in Japan have been always frowned on by conscientious people who tend to ignore or disrespect them. Consequently, both politics and religion have inevitably retained their life in name only. The reasons for progress in the Japanese economy and the decline in its politics and religion can be seen in various forms. But, in a word, it can be said to be because of the difference between the former's impersonal and latter's personal relations.

The Japanese are said to be the most skillful people in

the world in terms of cultivating the most refined things. I think behind their skill is found an abundance of sensuality in the minds of the Japanese. However, despite their skillfulness, foreigners will not respect Japanese trickery. They will only admire and respect the maker and the product when they are both good. It is natural to say that such a good man is raised through his religious faith. Conscientious people are yearning for a guiding principle through which such religious faith is fostered. The question is whether or not any established religions in Japan are fully realized and prepared for meeting this demand. If not, it is our task to work for this in the best possible way.

Looking at the present religious situation in Japan, we find lack of a clear vision and means on the side of the established religions to guide not only Japanese life and thought but also economy and politics. Therefore, we should re-establish an organization where a concrete system of thought is functioning in religious people from a well-defined guiding principle. We must have full confidence and pride in it. Such an organization would be established by those who look forward to the same goal in the same spirit. It seems that in the past the members of most established Japanese religions and academics have gone their own ways without mutual cooperation. If they do not have any concrete system of thought, the zeal and ability to guide conscientious people, they will be washed away by modern trends. If these three elements work together, people will be amazed at their great accomplishments.

Whichever elements we may have, we should re-affirm our faith and position, and with pride and confidence do our part to reorganize our religion for the betterment of our society.

෴ ෴ ෴

19. THE FUTURE OF BUDDHISM IN AMERICA

In this essay I would like to discuss the future of Buddhism in America in connection with the present situation of our missionary work.

In order to make the Buddhist missionary work in America effective, the following items should be provided, so that more people could be attracted to the Buddhist church and its activities: (1) The consolidation of better facilities, (2) the bringing up of better men (3) the promotion of better activities, and (4) the establishment of ways leading toward them.

(1) The Consolidation of Better Facilities

The present church is too small to accomodate the church activities well. Therefore, neighborhood land should be purchased and annexed to the church to build a mission school, library, cafeteria, oldmen's home, day-care center, hospital, gymnasium, social hall, student dormitory, recreation Hall, Japanese garden, cinerarium, guest room, and minister's residence. At the same time, the opening of branch temples in rural subdivision areas and a Buddhist University is urgently needed to meet the demands of our community. Also, the erection of a Japanese-style house with a tea room is strongly advised for the center of religious training.

(2) The Bringing up of Better Men

The resident ministers in the church should have a deep faith in Buddhism and protect the members spiritually. The directors should cooperate with the ministers and lead the rest of the members. The Board of Directors, led by the Bishop, should consist of two sub-boards, namely, the ministers' board and the laymen's board. The Board should appoint the directors of office management, service, research, promotion, and maintenance. Full-fledged ministers, assistant ministers, nuns, secretaries, and janitors should be hired and be better paid according to their capacities. Scholarship, training, sabbatical, pension and retirement system should be adopted so that incentive work and replacement can easily take place. Full-time directors should also be appointed by the Board for the mission school, oldmen's home, dormitory, day-care center, hospital, library, cafeteria and branch temples.

(3) The Promotion of Better Activities

The Sunrise service, Family service, Sunday service, Memorial Anniversary service, Wedding and Funeral services should be solemnly observed by the ministers and the members as well. All church members are requested to attend the Sunday services and participate in other church activities with the initiation of a Board,

Fujinkai, and YBA. The activities at various affiliated clubs should be encouraged so that they will have more membership and reputation. The Fujinkai (Junior and Senior) should have classes for Goeika singing, tea ceremony, flower arrangement, and handcraft, whereas the YBA (Junior, Intermediate and Senior) should have sport and social welfare clubs. The Sunday School should provide the systematic training course for the children with the help of the Fujinkai and YBA.

As for outside activities, ground-breaking, open house, hospital visitation, home visitation, public relations and personal counseling should be exercised more by the ministers. The publication of a Buddhist Bible, both in Japanese and English, will give the church members a better understanding of Buddhism and the principal of their way of life. Also through frequent distribution of materials (pamphlets and organ papers) the church activities can be made better known to the church members as well as the public. The church activities and sermons should be regularly broadcasted through daily newspapers, radio and TV, so that they can better inform the public, as well as tourists.

(4) The Establishment of Ways leading toward Them

In order to accomplish the above mentioned well, the bylaws for the church administration should be specified, so that the purpose and activities of the mission can be clarified. The direction of order and the separation of jobs should be enforced so that any division among the ministers can be avoided. As for the church finance, the membership fee should be raised and collected fully. The budget system should be adopted and the regular income be separated from the special income and donations. As for personal relations, the Board should appoint suitable men to the suitable places and let them make full use of their power and capacity. Ministers' and board meetings should be held frequently, so that the problems which arise may be dissolved quickly.

The above mentioned is the future image of the Buddhist church I have in my mind. When I look at the present situation of the Buddhist church activities in America, I see the generation of Japanese-Americans who are gradually replacing the first generation Japanese, and the difficult time the present church seems to have adjusting itself to its future development. In this transitional age, I wonder who can organize and direct the development program of the church, and interpret its policies and objectives to the members as well as to the public.

At this juncture, we are faced with the problem of either choosing a church which is closed to our ever-changing environment or the church which is always open and adjusting to it. If we determine to choose the latter, we must straighten out our work under the strong leadership of the Bishop and the Board of Directors, and endeavor for the betterment of the church by refraining from our indifference and selfish interest toward the church. I strongly urge all members "not to ask what the church can do for you, but to ask what you can do for your church."

Chapter 2

Buddhist Words of Wisdom

1. Every Day Is a Good Day

Yesterday is the bird which has already flown away; we should not worry about it. Tomorrow is the bird which is not yet caught; we should not yet worry about it.

Today! Today is the bird which we actually can grasp. We should not therefore kill this captured bird but make use of it. Yes, we should make use of today fully! Full of hope and thankfulness, we should make today meaningful by accomplishing our duty. Even if we die today, smilingly we should die. Today must be made into such a really valuable day.

2. Go Step By Step!

Those who conquered Mt. Everest never went up in one rush; they built a basecamp at the foot and started climbing inch by inch.

If you want to reach the goal you set forth, you should first accomplish that which you are undertaking, then go on to the next step. Follow hard workers, if you go forward step by step without rushing and yet without idling, the lofty peak will be yours soon.

3. Should You Complain?

Should you complain about your clothing? Should you complain about your food? Should you complain about your house?

Open up your inner eyes of thankfulness!

When you wear your clothes with thankfulness, when you eat with thankfulness, and when you dwell with thankfulness, you will always be happy.

How precious are the days we have. In contentment and appreciation, we should see everything happily and joyfully.

4. A True Human Being

Those who work unwillingly are like animals. Those who act upon orders are like prisoners.

Even though no one commands you, if you do what you believe is good, you are called a true human being.

Whatever your situation may be, if you try to do your best with hope and thankfulness, you are called a true human being.

5. Blame Yourself

Since you cannot control yourself by your own will, it is too much to expect others to be at your disposal.

Do you say that things will not turn out as you wish?

Do you say that others will not do as you wish?

Before you complain and blame others, you should blame yourself, such a powerless man as you are.

6. How Precious Is Our Life

A crane lives a thousand years and a tortoise more than a thousand years. Our life is only sixty years or so.

But we should not tick away our time by a man-made clock.

We are living this eternal now with ever-renewed wonder and inspiration.

It is a wonderful thing to be human!

7. Where Is Your Contentment

When summer comes, you wish to have winter, and when winter comes, you wish to have summer.

When you are single, you wish to get married, and when you are married, you wish to be alone.

Then where is your contentment? You are summing up your discontentment with your own will.

8. Are You Stubborn?

You must make an apology when you are at fault. Otherwise you will have an ache deep in your mind. Vomit the poison you have accumulated.

The more you do not regret your fault the more stubborn you will become.

Do not confuse stubborness with courage. The stubborn one persists in doing what he was turned down for. The brave one gets up after he has been turned down.

9. Speak Only of Today

We should never speak about yesterday. We should

never speak about tomorrow. We should only speak about today.

If we can do well today, we will be able to do well tomorrow.

Sometimes we may conquer a lofty peak; sometimes we may be submerged in the deep sea. Whatever may come, we are truthseekers and must do what we can today.

10. Work Silently

Do your own work silently even though no one is watching you. Do your own work silently even though no one is giving you credit.

Even if you are laughed at because of your foolishness, you should never give up your work, just do your work silently. If you do so decisively, you will accomplish even the hardest work with less fatigue and will unexpectedly gain support from others.

Try first, then behold the result.

11. Do We Really Love Others?

When we start boasting about ourselves, our loving-kindness shrinks. We dislike people because we do not appreciate them.

Through love, you appreciate people. Through appreciation, we love people.

12. A Mind Like the Ocean

If you drop a stone into the ocean, there would be no

stir in the water; but, if it be into a pool, there would be a wave in the water.

Likewise, if you are nervous about people's talk behind your back and become shaky, your mind is just like an easily stirred pool.

We should be bold enough to be just like the ocean.

13. *Pay Less and Buy More*

Nowadays, people seem to have more success without investing much effort; they want to make a profit with the least possible effort. It is foolish to think that ten dollars worth of commodity can be bought with a one dollar bill.

14. *A Happiness Maker*

We must be thankful when we wake up. We must be thankful when we take meals. We must be thankful while we work. We must be thankful when we go to bed.

When we are thankful, we are called a happiness maker.

15. *Our Vows*

Let us become a man to thoroughly believe in the goodness of others.

Let us become a man to share our accomplishment with others.

Let us become a man to take good care of our mental and physical health.

Let us become a man to think deeply over the matter we encounter.

Let us become a man to fulfil our task in life.

Let us become a man to enjoy the togetherness of life.

16. *Open Your Inner Eyes*

Those who have opened the inner eye say:

"Everyone treats us well. Wherever we go we are cheerful and happy. We are never tired of treading the journey of life."

Those who have not opened the inner eye say:

"Everyone treats us badly. Wherever we go, we are disappointed and unhappy. We are already tired of treading the journey of life."

17. *We Possessed Nothing*

When we were born, we possessed nothing. But, how much we have now! There are innumerable things which are called "mine". We should be thankful and should not be extravagant. When we were born, we possessed nothing.

18. *Do Not Despair*

When you find yourself in a deadlock, do not become impatient. Be patient. Tomorrow has its own wind.

Do not despair even though you have no confidence in tomorrow's work. The day after tomorrow is waiting.

Whatever things may be, they never remain still: they are constantly developing. The power is in your hand to change your situation; therefore, you should live with hope for the future.

19. *You Are Lucky*

You are lucky if you have a true friend with whom you can laugh and cry, and from whom you can get good advice to encourage you.

20. *Just Keep Smiling*

When we look at the mirror with a smiling face, the face in the mirror will also smile. When we look at the mirror with an angry face, the face in the mirror will also be angry.

We are just like mirrors. If we meet others with smiling faces, they will respond to us with smiling faces. If we meet others with angry faces, they will respond to us with angry faces.

21. *Each Step Is Important*

A is proceeding one step toward the East. B is proceeding one step toward the West. At first the difference is only two steps, but, as they step out further, the difference finally becomes hundreds of thousands of steps.

One step toward the Truth or False.

One step toward the Good or Bad.

One step toward the Beautiful or Ugly.

Do not say it is only one step. Each step is very important for us. In which direction is your step going?

22. *Wait for a Moment*

However heavy a burden you carry, you should never be discouraged. You should just endure hardship and never be crushed. The situation you encounter must be objectively taken into account, and you must make the utmost effort to face the situation.

23. *You Are What You Are*

If you are a cat, you should not try to resemble a lion. If you are a lion, you should not try to be like a cat. A cat is a cat, and a lion is a lion and nothing more. In itself is found the true value of each thing.

Feminine men and masculine women are both hateful.

24. *To Live or to Die*

He who lives only to wait for death is nothing but a creature who eats its own life.

He who make use of his own life fully and meaningfully is a creator who governs his own life.

Choose either way of life: the way to live or to die. It's up to you.

25. *Do not Pretend*

You will suffer if you pretend to do things beyond your capacity. You will be ashamed if you pretend to know what you actually do not know. You will be embarrassed if you pretend to possess the thing which you actually do not have.

Do not make unnecessary trouble by pretending.

26. *A Moment of No Return*

We never spend the same moment twice in our

journey of life. Then, how can we idle our time away! We should spend our time valuably and pleasantly. This moment comes only once in a life time.

27. *Praise and Respect*

Do you want to be praised? Reflect upon yourself first whether or not you deserve to be praised.

28. *Do not Be Vexed*

I was laughed at not because I did wrong, but because I did good. I was hated not because I did an evil deed, but because I did right. I was deceived not because I did a stupid thing, but because I did honestly.

29. *Pleasure After Bitterness*

When abused, do your own work instead of abusing others. When beaten do your own work instead of beating others. When kicked, do your own work instead of kicking others.

30. *True Appreciation*

Nowadays, everything is conveniently provided for us, and we do not pay any attention how it is given to us. We tend to think that we deserve to be given or else we can buy with money. In such ways, we can never feel appreciation to whatever is done for us.

31. *The Way to Become a Great Man*

When insulted, laugh it off! When kicked, just endure it! When overpowered, do not be crushed! It is painful

and vexing, but, I tell you, this is the same way great
men have passed.

32. *Only One Is Enough*

Only one is enough if you have a life-long task to
which you can dedicate yourself with a full heart.

Only one is enough if you have a bosom friend to
whom you can devote yourself in trust and respect.

Only one is enough if you have a good book that you
can read repeatedly to enrich your life.

33. *Do Positively!*

You will have a nervous breakdown if you bother
about trifles such as others' speaking ill of you behind
your back.

What matters is:

If you believe you are right, do positively what you
can!

There is no danger in treading the path alone as long
as you are right.

34. *When You Are Angry*

If you get angry, it is against your interests. If you are
wrathful, count from one to ten. If you are still wrathful,
repeat the Nembutsu ten times. If you are still wrathful,
go to bed and sleep. If you are still wrathful, go to a
mental hospital!

35. *As You Sow, So Shall You Reap*

Is there any such occasion that you sow the field with

melon and reap an egg-plant? A good cause produces a good effect, and an evil cause an evil effect. It is the never changing fact that you shall reap what you sow.

You must believe that if you do a good thing, you will never get unsatisfactory results.

36. We Are Alone

After all I must go alone on a journey of my life. The last citadel that I could retreat is nothing but mine.

I was born alone and I will die alone, leave alone and come alone.

How could I make myself cheap!

How could I neglect my precious life!

37. Pleasure After Work

Today I was busy all day long. Because of fatigue, I am able to sleep well. If we can sleep well, we shall be well awakened tomorrow. With clear eyes, we are able to work better.

May tomorrow be busy as well. Pleasure can be gained only after laborious work. This experience can never be appreciated by the idle man.

38. Are You Busy?

I cannot work well because I am busy. I cannot study well because I am busy. I cannot clean the room well because I am busy. Then, you cannot probably enjoy yourself well, because you are too busy.

39. Our Life Is Short

If we can live more than a hundred years, we might have time to get angry, envy, grieve and worry; but, regretfully, our life is too short to spend in such ways.

I am greedy to live out my short life fully so that I may not be able to make even a day meaningless.

How about you?

40. Take It Easy

It *does not* matter even if you fail a little bit. You should not be discouraged.

Stand up firmly and vigorously proceed two steps further.

Even though you retreat one step back, you will gain one step ahead if you proceed two steps.

41. We Are Not a God

We are not an almighty God; we are just human beings. Therefore, sometimes we make mistakes. We are not an insect nor an animal; we are just human beings. Therefore, sometimes we make mistakes.

42. Do not Hesitate

Make yourself lofty, clean and beautiful! The world of Truth, Goodness and Beauty is broad. Do not be reserved. Stretch out your arms to heaven.

43. Time Is Money

Yesterday is the light which is already burned out. Tomorrow is the light which is not yet turned on. Today is the light which is now burning.

Time is money: you have to make use of it just like the brilliantly burning light.

44. *Are You Shameless?*

You owe too much to the world, and yet do not pay back your debts: you are called "shameless."

45. *You Are Unlucky*

If you *do not* have any person who can scold and admonish you, you are unlucky. It is even dangerous because you are like an uncontrolled horse.

When you have those who can scold and admonish you, you should be thankful to them.

46. *You Are Happy*

You who complain about your unhappiness and yearn for happiness do need to change your attitude toward others.

Just open your inner eye, then you will be surprised to know that you are happy at the present.

Happiness and unhappiness are the products of your mind.

47. *Where Is Pleasure?*

I grieved at my unhappiness when I was eager to escape from suffering, and to gain pleasure. But, now I am very happy because I find pleasure in overcoming the suffering.

48. Going Our Way

We *do not* like to be an object of hatred, but there might be someone who hates us. We *do not* like to be an object of suspicion, but there might be someone who doubts us.

We have lots of things to say and to do: we are busy, but our life is too short. We have no time to curry favor with our superiors or defend ourselves.

We are going our way boldly enough. We have no regrets whenever we die.

49. Do not Be Enraptured

Do not become enraptured, because no kind of pleasure can continue forever.

Do not be discouraged, because no kind of despair can continue forever.

It is all right; you just stand firm!

50. You Are Already Happy

Do not think that you will become happy when your circumstances change. If you change your mind, your circumstances will be changed too.

Open your eyes and open your windows. The sun is already shining. Wake up your mind of contentment and open your mind of appreciation.

You are already happy.

51. Identify Yourself

Even though you think you are not stronger or not better than others, do not be ashamed of yourself. By trying to identify yourself with a stronger and better man whom you would like to be, you will become like him. Likewise, when you think and behave like a petty man, you will become like him in the course of time.

52. Pleasure in Life

As I am alone, I am really grateful when I encounter the people who are kind-hearted and reveal it to me. They make me think that I am no more alone.

53. What is Relief?

Sometimes we do not find anyone to whom we like to discharge our uneasy feelings. Sometimes we do not find anyone with whom we share our togetherness. In these occassions, our wretchedness and lonesomeness are more intensified than ever. However, we should never loose ourselves. We should objectively confront with the problems and patiently wait until the tide is over.

54. Adversity Makes You Wise

We reflect only when we are laughed at.
We become wise only when we are scolded,
And, we become strong only when we are beaten.

55. Give Nice Compliments to Others

Today, I am ashamed of not being able to do any good for others. What I can do is to give my nice compliments to them.

56. Do Not Pretend to Be Good

I do not like a man who pretends to be good.

He might say that he never did a wicked thing.

I think he is a liar. Since no one can judge himself through his eyes, how can he say he is good.

57. A Man of Men

If we are a man of men, we have to help those who are in need, keep a promise even though we are threatened to death, carry the heavy burdens as if nothing had happened, and keep smiling even though we are enraged. How about you?

58. Are you Bored?

Those who have no idea how the moon appeared, the flower bloomed, the birds sang and the insects twittered, would call this world as monotonous.

59. Embraced Life

You do not live, but someone makes you live.

Then, you would say, "I do live by myself".

Wait a moment. Who does make you live—you or your parents or others? We have to appreciate what makes us lead a happy life.

60. The Life of Thankfulness

I am very grateful to be able to work well, knowing that someone could not today. I am very grateful to be able to eat today, knowing that someone could not eat as much as I could. I am very grateful to be able to lead my life worthy enough today, knowing that someone could not but lead a disgusted life. I am very grateful to be able to sleep well, knowing that someone could not sleep at all.

61. Always Look Up the Bright Side

You must have missed the pleasant things if you think this world is full of suffering. You must have missed the convenient things if you think this world is full of inconvenience. You must have missed the kind men if you think this world is full of unkind men. If you try to look on the bright side of the world, you will find your life is worthy to live.

62. What a Pleasant Life!

When we are healthy, we should live up fully and significantly. When we are sick in bed, we should take a good rest under the doctor's care. And, when we are to die, we should be born into the Pure Land. What a pleasant life we are leading!

63. To which Do You Belong?

He is the best if he does not do any evil deed even though no one sees him. He is better if he does not do any evil deed when someones see him.

He is worse if he does a bad deed even though someone sees him. To which one do you belong?

64. Contentment and Discontentment

The fragrant flower blooms on the ground of grateful-

ness. The thorny flower blooms on the ground of discontentment. Which flower do you like better?

65. Truth Will be Revealed

I do not mind to be called foolish if I am not really.
I do not mind to be misunderstood if I am really right.
Let them call gold as brass.

The truth will be revealed sooner or later.

66. Ignore the Trifles

Even on this day, the fleeting wind flew and cold
water whirled. There were many unsatisfied and provok-
ing things to mention, but I ignored them all.

Today, I spent life pleasantly with thankfulness.

What a happy man I am!

67. Work Hard with Diligence

It is foolish to think of gaining fame without making
any effort. It is just like collecting shells while climbing a
mountain and picking mushrooms while entering the sea.

68. It is Up to your Mind

How tiny the house may be, it is a big home.
How big the house may be, it is a tiny home.
How dark the house may be, it is a bright home.
How bright the house may be, it is a dark home.
It is up to the minds of people who live there.

69. On Creativity

Picasso, world renowned painter, once said, "Creativity is a series of destructions". We really cannot create anything until we knock something else out of the way.

Therefore, we should not be content with what we have right now.

70. Encouragement and Comfort

Nowadays, many people doubt the existence of God or Buddha. It is natural to think that they are not existing in a physical sense. However, whenever we need some encouragement and comfort from someone, we acknowledge their existence. Without having such experience, we cannot find them at all no matter how intently and earnestly we seek them around us.

71. Balancing our Mind and Form

It has been said that our mind is subject to change according to our form, and vice versa. Without form, we are easily open to be subjective, emotional and pompous; without mind we become mechanical, frigid and oblivious to the needs of other people. We have to balance our mind and form to the extent that they will not conflict with each other.

72. Sublimate Yourself

When we stick to our materialistic desire, there seems no end to reaching our full satisfaction. Each time our desire is intensified and sometimes conflicts with others' desires. However, when we channel our desire into a spiritual one, we can fully satisfy our mind.

73. Express your Appreciation

When a wife was about to clean the empty lunch box brought back by her husband from work, she found a note in it that read, "This was the best lunch I have ever eaten. Thank you." As she read it, she was overwhelmed with joy, and completely forgot her weariness and boredom. No one will ever feel unpleasantness when praised by others.

Therefore, it is necessary for everyone to find something good in the other person and to express his sincere appreciation.

74. Noble Silence

When some people were busily engaged in small talk, the Buddha immediately stopped them and taught, "When the way-seekers assemble, there are two things to be discussed; either talk always about the Truth, or keep the noble silence."

75. No Wicked Man

In the book, "*Ethica Nicomachea*", Aristotle said, "the worst man is he who exercises his wickedness both towards himself and towards his friends, and the best man is not he who exercises his virtue towards himself but he who exercises it towards another; for this is a difficult task." There is no wicked man in the true sense of the word. A man is called or becomes "wicked" when he or others misjudge him.

76. No Recommendation in Life

Dr. Yoshimaro Toki once wished to enter the Zen monastery and asked his colleague, Master Beiho Taka-shina, for a letter of recommendation. However he received a surprising reply, saying, "You may go there anytime alone, without my letter. There will be no use for a nice letter in meditation." Dr. Toki reflected upon his foolishness and thanked him by saying, "You taught me a truth which I would never have learned even though I sat in meditation for years."

77. A Spiritual Gift

Once upon a time there was a man walking along a street one cold winter day. He came upon a beggar asking for alms. The beggar was old and dirty and was shivering in the cold. The man felt so sorry for the beggar that he searched in his pocket for something to give him. Since he had no money at that time, he felt so ashamed that he took hold of the dirty beggar's hand and offered his sympathy, apologizing for his lack of money. The beggar nodded and said, "You have given me a gift worth more than money." A warm handclasp given in sympathy was the best gift he could ever receive.

78. No One is Indispensable

There are people who boast that they are indispensable. They blame others for not doing any good and yet they claim that only by themselves will the work and job be well done. However, how many times in our daily lives have we seen people whom everyone thought were

hard to replace, had their jobs been taken over by someone else; and within a few days seen things going much
better than before. We are always being replaced by
someone who is just as good or even better.

79. *Move and Delay*

The art of living is deciding when to move and when
to delay. Many people like to settle the issue they confront in a hurried way. Here lies the pitfall in adventure.
Without making any haste, we have to look into the
actual situation and with sound judgement we must
decide whether to act or wait until the time is ripe.

80. *The Pleasure of Togetherness*

It has been generally said that when we are happy and
have someone to share it with, the pleasantness will be
multiplied, and when we are in sorrow and have someone to share it with, the sorrowfulness will be decreased.

One dying patient once confessed that he desparately
needed his bosom friend always beside him. We are
indeed frail beings so that we need someone to always
comfort or encourage us.

81. *Respect Yourself*

There are many people who simply cannot have faith
in the Supreme Being, because they have no faith in
themselves. They are so filled with self-doubt that they
cannot love themselves and have lost their self-esteem
through failure in life, through evil acts, and through

abuse from others. We must first accept ourselves and go on to live from there.

82. *Do not Make an Excuse*

When someone points out our mistakes, we often make an excuse in order to defend ourselves. And, instead of expressing our gratitude, we spare no pains to talk back against him, saying, "It is none of your business." It is not the way we should act.

We have to be grateful to him, understanding that out of his kind-heartedness he finds some hope in us, and is trying to make us better.

83. *Spring After Winter*

The bitterness of winter heralds the coming of spring. Likewise, the bitterness of our life experience is the pre-requisite for the spring of our life. A Japanese woman novelist, Yuriko Miyamoto, once wrote, "A peaceful spring has come after passing through the severe winter. A tiny flower of butterbur is born under the dew drops— after a long duration of harshness and wretchedness."

In our ups and downs of life, we should not confuse ourselves but look forward to the day when we can fully enjoy the spring of our life.

84. *Enjoy Your Life*

Our life is like dew drops which may fade away any moment. Why not enjoy such a short span of life fully and significantly. Forgetting oneself by means of drinking, shouting and yelling does not mean true enjoyment. Exposing oneself by means of gaining wealth, fame and power does not mean true enjoyment. Only when we reflect upon ourselves with deep insight and see that our temporal life is given, we are able to enjoy our life fully and significantly.

85. *Concentrate Your Mind*

Whenever we solve our problems, we have to understand what they are. The literal meaning of "understand" is "stand under". Facing the problem, we have to stand under and overcome it. Nasu-no-Yoichi, the Japanese classical archer-warrior, was once requested to hit the target on a floating boat. He could not first of all concentrate his mind because of his egoistic purposefulness. However, when he detached himself, and absorbed and became one with the target, he could release the shot and hit the target. This is not a mystical nor a speculative experience which only qualified men may acquire, but is a spontaneous experience which is manifested in our daily life.

86. *Open Your Eyes*

It has been said that the question mark is shaped like a hook because it is designed to catch information. The man who has lost the pleasure of fishing for answers is already developing his closed mind. We cannot enclose ourselves in the dim cell of our darkened world. Instead, we have to open our eyes to the wider world around us, so that we can see things as they really are and listen to something which is better than what we possess. Here is a good chance to develope our human capacity.

87. Man Versus Machine

In the midst of so-called modern society, we are apt to be tied up with telegrams, computer printouts, procedure materials, unnecessary correspondence, meetings, mail memoranda and aging files marked "Must Read". However, we cannot 100 per cent trust such means which are supposed to make us happy. One day, a wife received the telegram from her conventioneering husband, reading: "Having a wonderful time. Wish you were her". An error of one letter of word plunged the wife into despair. We must be aware that the machine was made for man, not man for the machine.

88. Win Rightly

In order to win we have to win rightly. By winning over against others, it should encourage others to make further progress. It is not good merely to win in order to negate others' progress. The Japanese swordman Musashi Miyamoto, while he was young, felt the pleasure of winning by killing others. However, as he grew older, he never killed his enemies until they realized the inferiority of their skills.

89. Do not be Disillusioned

There is a Japanese saying, "the lady looks pretty when we look at her at night or from a distance or under the parasol." I believe there is some truth in this saying. Likewise almost everything looks green when we look at them over the hedges. However, when we approach them and take a close look, we are sometimes discouraged. Even the men of dignitaries, when we look at them through their pictures, writings or books, appear great. But when we meet them, we are sometimes discouraged. Therefore, we must take a close look and see who they really are in order to respect what they have done.

90. Be Excellent!

We have to respect anyone's competence including our own. The excellence of anything we have engaged in not only helps us but also others. I know a company executive who only employs men of excellence. He says that only the excellent man could promote his company's progress. Excellence is the best in the trade, says a Chicago high-school junior, "I'd even respect an excellent thief!"

91. We Can Do It

It has been said that a man like Mr. Shoichi Yokoi who had lived alone in the jungles for more than 28 years could survive because of his wisdom to maneuver the situation he confronted and his eagerness to live with renewed hope, courage and confidence.

A man can do the unbelievable thing only when he is obliged and determined to do so in the most crucial situation. However, the man like us who has been pampered and warmly protected by the environment is spoiled and will easily "crack himself up."

92. Positive Thinking and Doing

Do not pray for easy lives. Pray to be though and

strong. If you pray for tasks equal to your powers, you will be submitted under their control, and no more be called as a true human being.

93. *Suffering Is Bliss*

Nowadays, many people doubt that life has any meaning. They do not know what they want to do, and are easily led by what other people want them to do, thus completely succumbing to conformism.

Dr. Viktor E. Frankl, a noted Viennese psychiatrist said that "Life can be made meaningful by what we give to the world in terms of our creation; by what we take from the world in terms of our experience; and by the stand we take toward the world, that is to say, by the attitude we choose toward suffering."

94. *Become a Specialist*

When we ask something of the specialist which we cannot do by ourselves, we are amazed at his fine skill. Whatever it may be—design, construction or repair work—it is well done once in the hands of the specialist. Of course, the specialist has the materials and tools which we do not possess, but because of his skill he can handle the seemingly impossible in an efficient way. Someone said that one becomes wise because of his profession. One's skill benefits himself and contributes to his society at large.

95. *Keep On With Our Work*

It is a general trend that even though at first we show

enthusiasm in anything we undertake, within a few days we lose interest and soon give it up. Many of our new projects such as keeping a diary or publishing periodicals, have thus been discontinued in the course of time. We should always prop up our works with renewed hope and courage so that they will become a part of our habit.

96. *Avoid Imitations*

Nowadays, the reproductions of fine arts are so flourishing in the world market that they are hardly distinguishable from the genuine ones. Their prices are reasonable enough to one's reach and their effects are as good as the genuine ones. However, when we are always satisfied with the imitations, we gradually lose our interest in finding the good quality of genuine ones, and even lose our sense of evaluation.

97. *Attached Detachment*

In our daily living, we should concentrate ourselves on the problem we are engaged in, and yet not be swayed by it. When we are too much involved in it, we tend to lose our sight and easily fall under the yoke of irresistible habits. Thereafter, we should not be freed from attachment.

98. *Do Not Confront In the End*

In our daily life, we tend to put off our assigned works until the very last moment and then finish them. Likewise, when we are driven into a tight corner, we can do almost anything we want. Therefore, it is good to think that we always face a crisis. However, for a fugitive who has taken a hostage, the problem is something different. We must ignore him or give him ample time to think over his misbehavior. If we press him close, and do not find him a way of escape, he will commit any manner of unbelievable thing.

99. Four Sorts of Men

There are four sorts of men in the world. The first is he who makes both himself and others unhappy; he is a fool, guide him. The second is he who makes himself happy and others unhappy; he is selfish, teach him. The third is he who makes others happy and himself unhappy; he is naive, wake him. The fourth is he who makes both himself and others happy; he is wise, respect him.

100. How To Die Peacefully

It has been said that a man who encounters his own death wishes to experience almost everything and have someone always beside him. He also goes through five emotional states: shock, fear, anger, "bargaining with God or Buddha" and final resignation.

What he needs is a good counselor who will allow these emotions to be expressed and will comfort him saying that death is a kind of long, painless sleep. Once he has such faith, he can overcome his death honestly and successfully.

Chapter 3

True Buddhist Stories

1. DO THINGS PROMPTLY

Once upon a time, a Buddhist master, nicknamed Thunderbolt, lived at Heirinji Temple, 15 miles west of Tokyo. One day a samurai visited the temple and met him in a room with the question, "What are you doing here?" Immediately, the master stood up and kicked him out. Astonished and in a rage, the samurai put his hand on his sword and was about to kill him. At this moment, a monk quietly entered the room and offered him a cup of tea. However, trembling, the samurai poured out the tea on the floor. The master asked him, "What are you doing now?" The samurai could not answer the question, and instead his eyes goggled. The master said smilingly, "When the tea is spilled, we wipe it up," and he cleaned the floor with a cloth. The humiliated samurai admitted his defeat and hurriedly left the temple.

We can learn from this story the importance of quickly doing the right thing at the right time.

ᖰ ᖰ ᖰ

2. BEYOND LOVE AND HATE

In a remote village of the Yaba valley in Kyushu, a Buddhist travelling monk arrived in 1724. He was watching a funeral service which was dedicated to a man who had fallen from a cliff and died. He was told that people often died when they attempted to cross the mountain to go to the other villages. He went to see the pathway which went along the cliff, and came back with a decision. Then the news spread that he was going to dig a tunnel underneath. The villagers only laughed away the project, and paid no attention to him. But before long the sound of a hammer echoed; he had begun to dig out the cliff, inch by inch.

From morning till night, he never tired of hacking out the rocks. It was a slow progress. A year went by, but the sound of hammering did not cease. Two years, three years, and four years passed, and the monk still did not stop his hammering. Three more years went by and only one-third of the tunnel was dug. Villagers began to feel ashamed for letting him dig alone, and joined the project. However, they fell off from the party within a year or two. He looked pale and his cheeks were sunken, and yet he never gave up digging. Eighteen years had passed by since he had begun to dig, but only half of the distance was covered.

One day, a young samurai, named Saburobei, came up to the village searching for the monk. Saburobei's father had been killed by this monk before he had entered the priesthood, when he was himself a samurai employed by Saburobei's father. Saburobei's father had kept a concubine in his house. One day this concubine fell in love with the samurai who later became this monk. Hearing this, Saburobei's father summoned the then samurai and beat him severely. As Saburobei's father was about to kill him with a sword, the samurai grabbed a candlestick that was close by in self defense, and by mistake, stabbed Saburobei's father and killed him. Since then, Saburobei had been pursuing the monk, searching for vengeance. Saburobei went to see the monk and confronted the enemy that he had been searching for many years. Knowing that some day Saburobei would come for revenge, the monk was ready to meet the sword. However, by this time the tunnel was nine-tenths done, and the villagers, gathered around, and begged the samurai to wait until the tunnel was completed. Saburobei accepted their petitions unwillingly and waited for five days, burning the fire of vengeance in his mind. Finally he could not wait any longer, and one dark night he sneaked out from his bed, and dashed to the tunnel to try to kill the monk. But hearing in the darkness the sound of the monk chanting Buddhist scriptures, he felt something and drew back quietly.

A few days passed, and Saburobei joined the digging with the monk. The old monk held up his hammer and hacked away the stone with Saburobei's help. They worked together day and night which quickened the completion of the tunnel. And it was on September 10, 1746 that a vague light pierced through from the other side of the tunnel: it was finally completed after twenty laborious years of work. The monk put down his hammer and said to Saburobei, "Now is the time to kill me" . . . There was a silence, and now, instead of taking up his sword, Saburobei bent before the old monk, and took his hand while his eyes became full of tears. After a short while they emerged from the tunnel. It was a beautiful night; a full-moon was smilingly gazing down upon them.

∾ ∾ ∾

3.   A TEAR DROP REFORMS A MAN

Ryokan was born in a poor village of Niigata in 1758. He was not known to the public until his Haiku poems became famous among poetry-lovers. At the age of 21 he became a Buddhist monk, and after the streneous work of sitting at Entsuji temple for seventeen years, he returned home, and lived in a small hut in the midst of Mt. Kunigami. He had a nephew named Umanosuke who was always drinking, gambling, and fighting, and no one could control him. One day, Umanosuke's parent begged him to stay at their home and to council Umanosuke. So Ryokan stayed at their home receiving warm treatment in every way possible.

More then ten days passed, and yet Ryokan gave Umanosuke neither instruction nor remonstration. The parents were vexed, and one day went to his room requesting him to give remonstration. However, they found Ryokan playing with some lice on the veranda. They thought he was crazy after having done severe training in the temple, and asked him to leave the house.

Next morning, when Ryokan was about to leave the house, Umanosuke was asked to send him off to the hut, and as Umanosuke was busy tying his sandle-strings, he felt something warm drop on his neck. Umanosuke looked up and saw Ryokan gazing at him with tears in his eyes and with a look kinder than that of his parents. Then they headed toward Ryokan's home. While they were travelling on foot, Ryokan said just a few words, "Umanosuke, you must be lonesome. I was too when I was your age. Write a poem and bring it to me if you wish." Thereafter, Umanosuke's personality changed completely.

ဢ ဢ ဢ

4. THE LIFE OF A CRIPPLED LADY

A few years ago, an old Japanese Buddhist monk visited the United States at the invitation of the Federal Government. He travelled around the States and met many Americans. Whereever he went, he spoke with his charming manner and collection of pictures. The pages were covered with many tiny pictures of a smiling Buddha. The monk explained how he had come to carry these pictures.

Way back in 1929 he was residing in a mountain temple of Japan. One day he received a beautiful woman visitor who was almost in her thirties. She told him about her misfortune. Until that time she had had nothing to worry about in her life. She was born into a well-to-do family and there were many expectations for her future life: marriage, children, and a restful life. However, all of a sudden misfortune overtook her: her body was completely paralyzed from head to toe and she could only use her hands. Hope for her was given up by all the doctors, who said that her life would only last for a month or so. She called on the monk to hear what advice she could possibly get. The monk paused for a while and then gave her instructions; namely, to draw with Chinese ink a picture of a smiling Buddha one million times. She first hesitated to accept the advice because it seemed too much for her. However, she thought it might guarantee her life until she completed them, and finally accepted.

From that time on, she never grew weary of drawing the same picture from morning till night, and never for a single day did she ever stop. It continued for more than 30 years. She drew and drew and each time for her the drawing was the first and last of her life; she gradually began to feel the joy of living despite of her ill-fated fortune. The more she could draw and live another day, the more she felt a gain in life. On an August day in 1959, she finally finished her work, and with joy she was taken to visit the now old monk at his temple. Both of them were overjoyed with the happy reunion, and, moreover, the completion of the promised drawings.

When he decided to go to America, the monk requested the lady to lend him the pictures, and took them with the wish to share with others the same spirit she had received. The monk and the lady are now more than 70 years of age, and yet are still healthy and joyful.

She wants to continue her drawing until the final moment of her life, although she long ago completed the millionth drawing. She is still doing it somewhere in Japan.

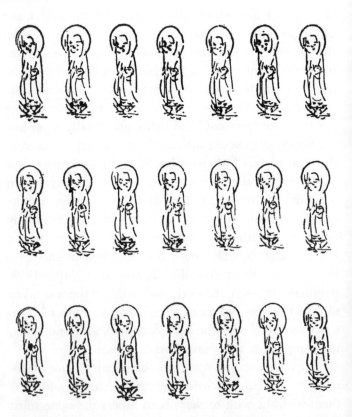

The picture shown above is drawn by the crippled lady introduced in this chapter.

5.   THE CONDUCT OF UNSELFISHNESS

A few years ago, the ship S.S. Tokiwamaru was reported to have sunk in a whirlpool of Naruto Strait off Kobe, Japan. On board that ship was Mr. Inubushi who happened to meet a boy at the port who was entrusted to him by the child's mother since he was traveling alone for the first time. Mr. Inubushi and the boy were enjoying the trip as the ship ran smoothly in the Inland Sea. However, on the following day, the ship was unexpectedly sunk at 1:00 a.m. off Kobe. Inubushi encouraged the boy in the dark and cold night sea. They swam together until finally Mr. Inubushi found a rescue boat nearby. After he saw that the boy was saved, his energy was exhausted and he disappeared into the dark sea. Upon hearing this news, many people all over Japan were impressed by this heart-warming story, and sent letters of sympathy with some monetary gifts to the bereaved family. However, instead of keeping the money for themselves, the family donated the money to social welfare work to be used for more depressed people.

そ そ そ

6.   BE CAUTIOUS BEFORE ANYTHING HAPPENS

There is a story about the sword master, Bokuden Tsukahara, who lived in Japan about 300 years ago. One day when one of his disciples was passing by a horse, the horse was about to kick him. He dodged the horse by a second, and his skill was praised by the near-by people who thought he should be deserved to be called the true disciple of Bokuden Tsukahara. However, only Tsukahara looked displeased and scolded him. Master Tsukahara said, "The horse has the nature of kicking out at anything approaching. Your skill is still immature for not knowing this fact. You must be cautious before anything happens." Those who have trained their skills for emergency use would praise Tsukahara's disciple for his quick action. However, Tsukahara taught the way of avoiding any accident before it happens. Therefore, even for us, we must take thorough precaution before we must take any quick action in an emergency.

ᐒ ᐒ ᐒ

7.　MOTHERLY LOVE TOWARD A SON

Once upon a time, there were a young man and his old mother in Nagano Prefecture, Japan. In those days, it was the custom to abandon old mothers in a remote place of Mt. Ubasute. One day a young man decided to abandon his old mother and left his home with her. On the road to the mountain, the old mother, while being carried on her son's back, snapped the tree branches above her and threw them on the path. The son, recognizing that his mother's exercise would become a guide post to her way back from the mountain, scattered them away one by one. Soon they arrived at the place of no return on the mountain, he took his mother down from his back and was about to leave the place. The old mother said to him, "My dear son, I left the tree branches on the road in order that you may find the way to return home safely." The son felt so sorry for his selfish thought and conduct and was impressed by the deep compassion of his mother toward him. Therefore, completely reformed in his mind, he took his mother back home and showed filial piety to his mother in every respect.

ﾟ ﾟ ﾟ

8.   THE VIRTUOUS MAN FINALLY WINS

A long time ago in a village in Japan, there lived three brothers, named, Rikibei, Tomizo and Jinkichi. The eldest brother Rikibei was physically strong and always held down the other brothers by force. The second brother, Tomizo, in his vexation, made up his mind to become a rich man so that he could win over his brothers. As the time went on, Tomizo accumulated enough money to build many houses and began to look down on his brothers. By this time, the physical strength of the eldest, Rikibei, was declining, and being badly off, he inevitably begged Tomizo for shelter. The youngest, Jinkichi, was a gentle and nice boy. With the idea of saving others, he studied medicine diligently and after becoming a surgeon, opened a hospital in his village. However, none of the villagers, who were stricken with superstition, cared for his scientific treatment. He lived very poorly and yet never gave up his strong belief in medical science. One day, as Tomizo's house caught on fire, both Rikibei and

Tomizo were burnt out and came under Jinkichi's care. At that time, an epidemic was spreading among the villagers, and those who obeyed Jinkichi's advice were cured while those who did not rapidly died. This time, the villagers and Jinkichi's two brothers finally came to realize that Jinkichi's effort was stronger and more valuable than anything else, and they honored him as a saviour of the village.

Chapter 4

The Significance of Pure Land Buddhism

In the West, much has been discussed about the significance of Zen Buddhism by a number of able exponents like Daisetz Suzuki or Alan Watts, but little is known of its counterpart, namely Pure Land Buddhism which is also of vital importance to the formation of Japanese spirituality as the core of its culture. It is mainly because there are few exponents of Pure Land Buddhism familiar to us, and at the same time, its superficial resemblance to Christianity does not seem to attract us. However, Zen is the Buddhism of the intellectual, and Pure Land is the Buddhism which took the general masses of the Japanese into its fold. There has been no other Buddhist invocation which has endeared itself to the Japanese people as much as "Namu Amida Butsu" and more than half of the entire Japanese population have been embraced by the teaching of Pure Land Buddhism. Therefore, it is safe to say that Pure Land thought is the core of Japanese culture which remain the same, while retaining the differences which vary throughout the ages. In this respect, we must pay more attention to the study of Pure Land Buddhism as expounded by Honen.

Nowadays, despite the criticism that the Western journey to the East is a search for the occult, the magical, the bizarre, the exotic, or the beyond-morality life styles, there are increasing numbers of Westerners who are unable to identify themselves with any norms or value orientations of their traditional society. The old norms have been undermined, or have become outmoded. The exitement, pleasure and fulfilment that can come from serving a higher purpose than the material satisfaction of self appear to be missing. Therefore, they have departed at their own will in search of a new and meaningful way of life. Erich Fromm once wrote, "Ours is a life not of brotherhood, happiness, contentment, but of spiritual chaos and bewilderment dangerously close to a state of madness—not the hysterical kind of madness which existed in the Middle Ages but a madness akin to schizophrenia in which the contact with inner reality is lost and thought is split from affect." We can well understand this chaotic situation when we look at the recent occurrences of racial and student riots, hijackings or innocent murders, and the popularity of juvenile delinquency, drug addiction or occult practices in our daily life. All these phenomena have materialized as a result of our losing sight and direction not only on the personal but also on the national front, and we are gradually being alienated from ourselves, from our fellow men, and from nature.

The situation was almost the same at the time Honen appeared as it is now. In the Kamakura period of Japan in the 12th century, people's lives were constantly threatened by a series of epidemics, natural disasters and civil wars. Hypocrisy prevailed among the people, and only a handful of privileged people could enjoy the splendor and luxury of sophisticated life. The rest of the people were burdened with heavy taxes and low incomes. In order to survive the struggle of existence, they lived at the sacrifice of others by fighting and killing each other. The power of the ruling classes shifted from one to another, and yesterday's friends became today's enemies. There was no mutual trust or respect at all. Seeing this desperate situation, concerned people were greatly discouraged and deeply felt the uncertainty of life.

It was in this period that a drastic change took place in the field of religion. When Honen appeared and initiated the new teaching, Buddhism became for the first time the religion of the masses, and has contributed to the formation of Japanese spirituality as the core of its culture. Therefore, I believe it is extremely important for us to re-evaluate the significance of Pure Land Buddhism expounded by Honen, although we are far from the Kamakura period in which he lived culturally, geographically and chronologically. The reason is that by learning Pure Land Buddhism we can not only grasp the essence of Japanese spirituality but also deepen and widen our horizons in order to give our lives a more concrete reality and to make our lives ultimate and meaningful in this time of turmoil.

First of all, let us focus our attention to the significance of Honen's life history (cf. The first chapter of Part 3), and notice the three distinguishable stages which developed in his career, and were at work in his thoughts, attitudes and acts.

In the first stage, between 1141 and 1175, Honen

studied very hard, trying to absorb all the existing teachings of his time on Mt. Hiei in order to gain salvation for his own sake. During this period, he was believed to have read through the large collection of Buddhist scriptures, called *Tripitaka*, and their commentaries three times, and was called the most learned man on Mt. Hiei. He once confessed that, "Never does a single day pass that I do not read the scriptures. Only one day I missed, and that was the day that Kiso Kanja invaded the capital." However, one day when he was staying in Kyoto, Honen met a priest from Mt. Hiei who asked him on what scripture he had founded the Jodo denomination. He replied, "On that passage in Shan-tao's commentary on the Meditation Sutra." Hearing this, the priest said, "Do you mean to say that a single passage such as this was enough to establish a new denomination?" Honen only smiled and made no reply. When this priest went back to Mt. Hiei, he told his master that Honen did not give him any answer, and the master said, "That was because the question did not deserve an answer. The fact is that Honen is not only fully acquainted with the Tendai, but he extended his studies to all other teachings, and has a deep knowledge of them far better than anyone else. So do not delude yourself by imagining he did not answer because he was not able to."

In the second stage, between the time of his initiation of new teaching in 1175 and the time of his remission from exile in 1211, Honen persuaded the people of all classes and tried to transfer his acquired merit of salvation to others through his compassionate thought and action. One day he was called upon by a warrior named Naozane Kumagai, who excelled in fighting and killing enemies in battle, and who confessed his past committed sins to him. Hearing this, Honen never blamed him for his sins, but told him that he only needed to gain salvation through the calling of the Nembutsu whole-heartedly. Naozane was overjoyed to hear it and completely changed his mind thereafter, and became an earnest disciple of Honen. Another time, when Honen was on his way to exile, he met a couple of old fishermen who asked him, "From childhood it has been our business to take the lives of fish for our living. Now as we are told that people who kill living things must go down to hell and suffer there, we want to know if there isn't some way of escaping from this?" Honen replied kindly, "If you but repeat the Nembutsu, you will be born into the Pure Land by virtue of Amida Buddha's merciful Vow." Hearing this, they shed their joyful tears and joined in his fold.

In the third stage, Honen appreciated the merits of the teaching of Pure Land Buddhism which were inter-acting and inter-penetrating between him and his disciples for the rest of his life until he passed away in 1227. During this period, he stressed the importance of calling the Nembutsu as much as possible. He once said, "Numbers are not necessarily essential, but there is a need for constant calling of the Nembutsu. If a definite number of repetitions is not prescribed, it might lead to negligence. Large numbers of repetitions are therefore advised."

Honen deeply perceived the frailty of human nature, so that he recommended the simple means of calling the

Nembutsu for the common people, and joined together the cognitive, the affective and the directive elements of human nature into one. He firmly believed that with the full participation of our thought, feeling and action we are able to attain and appreciate the preciousness of a healthy and sound way of life. Thus, Honen was indeed a man of clever mind, gentle disposition and strong character. He was stern with himself, striving after a strict observance of Nembutsu practice, and was tolerant toward others, recognizing the differences of human ability, character and situation. While he was in fact, as his name Honen suggest, 'A Master of Great Harmony with Nature', he had keen insight to choose the most essential thing for salvation and a wealth of warm human affection; and his happy blending of purity and compassion attracted many people of different classes surrounding him. He was actually a man who transcended himself in the sacred world, and yet he was satisfied with himself as a commoner in the profane world. He refused official titles and degrees, although ironically he was most often given the honorary titles, called *Daishigo*, from the succeeding Japanese Emperors. Therefore, Honen's burying place is very symbolic. When he passed away, he was buried at the site of Seishido in the compound of Chion-in Temple, the headquarters of the Jodo denomination, which is situated in the middle of Mt. Hiei, the sacred place of Japanese Buddhism, and in the bustling downtown Kyoto, the center of profane world.

Then, what does the teaching of Pure Land Buddhism, expounded by Honen, contribute to the formation of

Japanese spirituality. To give an answer to this question, I would like to point out three characteristics of Pure Land Buddhism which have influenced the Japanese, namely, the realistic, all-embracing and substantial.

In the first place, it has been generally said that Japanese culture was stimulated by one foreign culture after another—Buddhist, Confucian, Taoist, European and American cultures—and made use of them as catalysts to its own formation. The Japanese consistently sought models outside Japan and created the composite whole of their culture by absorbing, but not being swallowed by the foreign elements. They transformed and adapted to their special needs and tastes. They never took one element as absolute, or excluded others. This was due to the fact that Japan is an isolated country which became unified very early as a nation, with one race and one common language. These geographical and historical conditions resulted in the formation of one homogeneous culture and retained harmony among the people. Therefore, some scholars contend that Japanese culture is multi-layered, or Japan absorbed foreign elements like a sponge, but they were skin-grafts which though eagerly accepted, never became a core of the Japanese value pattern, but were rather co-existing superficially with other heterogeneous elements. I think this concept of retaining harmony within, and becoming curious about anything new and different from outside and absorbing it open-mindedly, only if they are worthy and applicable to the Japanese, was mainly nourished by the realistic teaching of Pure Land Buddhism.

In the second place, Honen insisted that men are common mortals who have many worries and troubles and cannot escape from committing sin. He was acutely aware of his passion-ridden nature and the impossibility of purifying his spirit except for the assurance of rebirth in the Pure Land given by Amida Buddha. He deeply perceived that in this profane world, nothing is permanent, but perishable instead. Therefore, for the Japanese, to be born into the Pure Land after life is so assured by the saving power of Amida Buddha that they have been rather optimistic about their present life, no matter how horrible it may be, and there have been few class conscious or racial crises in Japan. This has been true up to the present time. I think this concept was mainly nourished by the all-embracing teaching of Pure Land Buddhism.

In the third place, Honen once said, "Even while engaging in worldly affairs, you should always act in the Nembutsu, not take the Nembutsu as a subsidiary means." He emphasized that to work hard in worldly affairs is no vice at all. Instead of sitting in meditation, as in the case of Zen Buddhism, Honen stressed the calling of the Nembutsu whether walking or standing, sitting or lying. It requires the full participation of our mental, emotional and physical strength. Therefore, in later years in the Tokugawa period, Shosan Suzuki, one of the Pure Land followers, said, "If the farmers can make a vow to refrain from attachment, and dig the land with the calling of the Nembutsu, they will surely be born into the Pure Land." Another Pure Land devotee, Saichi, said,

"My mind only is everything. It is filled up with so many evil thoughts, but with all its evil thoughts, it is brimming with Namu Amida Butsu." For him, everything was dissolved in the Nembutsu: his life began with the Nembutsu and ended up in the Nembutsu. This is neither a mystical nor a speculative experience which only qualified men may acquire, but is a spontaneous experience which is acquired by any men. These men gradually transformed the teaching of Nembutsu which was once confined in the domain of the sacred world to the profane world, and made it applicable to our daily living. Such practical application of the Nembutsu into worldly affairs was mainly nourished by the substantial teaching of Pure Land Buddhism.

It was because of these realistic, all-embracing and substantial teachings of Pure Land Buddhism that Japan was able to modernize her country without much strife and to develope a way to cope with what Max Weber called the secularization of Protestant Christianity. This is evident in the fact that despite her complete surrender to the Allied Nations in 1945, the Japanese spirituality did not change much, and miraculously revived within a short period and has been maintained with slight modifications to the present day. Every country has its merits and demerits, and Japan certainly has her demerits. Although she retains her domestic harmony, she is not good at establishing international communications or contributing to international harmony, since she has been in isolation for a long time. Therefore, she should pay more attention to the outside, and contribute to world peace with her realistic, all-embracing and substantial teachings.

Then, what elements can we draw from the teaching of Pure Land Buddhism for the enrichment of our way of life? Of all the characteristics of Pure Land Buddhism, there are many things which we can learn from them, but this time I would like to point out only three things: namely, the teaching of identity experience, personal encounter, and religious practice.

In the first place, Pure Land Buddhism teaches us the importance of realizing the Oneness of all life. Nowadays, the preoccupation with our own 'soul' frequently makes us selfish and 'rugged individuals' and too often obscures our vision of the Oneness of all life. Increasing urbanization and geographic mobility have strained or broken our social ties which hold us together, give warmth to human relationships, and assure each individual a place and a personal identity with society. Therefore, we tend to feel rootless, not deeply involved with the people who live around us. If we understand the importance of the Oneness of all life, we can regain our mutual respect and share happiness with each other since we are one and the maltreatment of another is none other than the maltreatment of ourselves. This concept does not mean that we are arranged in a row at the bottom level, but by eliminating all the selfish attachment from us, and by admitting the differences of characters and capabilities, we can fully make ourselves unique human beings.

In the second place, Pure Land Buddhism teaches us the importance of personal encounter with others. Nowadays, our unique personalities and characters have been obscured because of the development of modern technology and mass production which have taken over man's job and position. We tend to become bystanders and irresponsible for what we have done and are doing, and our personal relationships between men are scarce. The mutual trust and respect as possessed by Honen for his master Shan-tao, and Shinran for his master Honen, are hardly seen among people today. Only our close ties seem to be knitted by bonds of depriving or being deprived materially. Therefore, we are gradually being alienated from ourselves, from our fellow men and from our society. What we need is not impersonal or hypocritical relationships between men, but personal and intimate relationships which will elevate ourselves together in order to reveal the infinite possibilities of our innate Buddha-nature.

In the third place, Pure Land Buddhism teaches us the importance of doing religious practices which require the full participation of our mental, emotional and physical strength. Honen once said, "I have been repeating the Nembutsu as much as possible." When he went out, instead of taking a carriage, he always went on foot, wearing straw sandals. On the contrary in our affluent society we are conveniently provided with many modern contrivances which shorten our labor and save time, and hardly consume our energies in order to maintain a natural and reasonable metabolic rate. One day my medical doctor told me that we are so over-fed and stuffed with lots of foods and sweets that we will become fat and suffer from avoidable illnesses, and consequently shorten our lives at our own will. We are spoiled because we try to avoid working ,as much as possible, and instead prefer to take rests or spend easy and carefree lives. Honen warned that in such a life we can never appreciate the preciousness of life, and never become healthy and sound in mind and body. Recently I read in a weekly magazine, saying that in Los Angeles a drive-in church has opened and attracts many audiences on Sundays who sit back in their comfortable cars and listen to the sermon delivered through the microphone. I wonder how they can receive the blessing of God through mere listening to the Word of God on the air. There is a saying, "Religion lies more in walk than in talk." Whichever the case may be, in religious or secular exercises, I believe that only after we challenge, endure and surmount the obstacles and hardships which we set upon in our spiritual and physical lives, can we really appreciate a meaningful way of life.

Although many things may differ between Honen's time in the Kamakura period of Japan and our contemporary age, there are certain things which seem to resemble each other with more tenseness and urgency. Therefore, it is my conviction that in this time of crisis and confusion, Pure Land Buddhism expounded by Honen will throw new light on the nature of man and heighten the sense of what it is to think, what it is to feel, and what it is to do. It will also help those who suffer and yet try to live better, to regain the once-lost confidence, strength and hope. It will also guide those who fall into the false intellectualizations which are the natural result of experience based on the subject-object split in Western civilization.

APPENDIX

APPENDIX.

What to Read on Buddhism

An increasing number of Westerners have become interested in Buddhism, and I have often been asked about English books on Buddhism suitable for the general reader. There are countless numbers of translated scriptures and commentaries on these scriptures, however they are rather difficult reading for the beginner. The reader may start with any of the books on this list but I suggest that he read one or two from the introductory section first.

A. *Introductory Books on Religion*

1. THE INDIVIDUAL AND HIS RELIGION, by Gordon Allport (The Macmillan Co., New York, 1950)

   A psychological interpretation of the individual's relationship to his religion. This is a valuable book because the author distinguishes the religion of maturity from the religion of a child.

2. MAN FOR HIMSELF, by Erich Fromm (Rinehart & Company, New York, 1947)

   In this interesting book a psychoanalyst takes up

the problem of ethics and values which he believes must be faced in order to achieve a complete understanding of personality and human potentiality.

3. DYNAMICS OF FAITH, by Paul Tillich (Harper & Brothers, Paperback, New York, 1959)

"There is hardly a word in the religious language, both theological and popular, which is subject to more misunderstandings,—than the word "faith." Today the term "faith" is more productive of disease than of health. It confuses;—creates alternately skepticism and fanaticism, intellectual resistance and emotional surrender, rejection of genuine religion and subjection to substitutes." This stimulating book is a must for those interested in the role of religion in our time.

4. RELIGION WITHOUT REVELATION, by Julian Huxley (Harper & Brothers, New York, 1958)

Julian Huxley is a distinguished biologist. It is particularly interesting to learn what a naturalist thinks about religion.

5. TAO OF SCIENCE, by R.G.H. Siu (The Massachusettes Institute of Technology Press, Cambridge, 1957)

The author shows how Eastern ways are modified

in the process of being Westernized and how, at the same time, Eastern wisdom has come to affect the Western scheme of things. He is a Chinese American scientist who has a warm understanding of both cultures.

B. *Introductory Books on Buddhism*

1. BUDDHISM IN GENERAL

1. *LIGHT OF ASIA,* by Edwin Arnold (Jaico Books, Calcutta, 1949)
   In this poem, the life of the Great Sage was sympathetically presented to the West for the first time. The book was written nearly 100 years ago and has become one of the world classics.

2. *GOSPEL OF BUDDHA,* by Paul Carus (Open Court Publishing Co., Chicago, 1943 reprint)
   This can be regarded as a Buddhist Bible for the general reader. It deals with the Buddha's life and his teachings simply and lucidly.

3. *LIFE OF BUDDHA,* by Edward Thomas (Routledge & Kegan Paul, London, reprint 1956)
   This is a scholarly work on the life of the Buddha, which all advanced students should read.

4. *THE LIFE OF THE BUDDHA,* by A. Foucher (Wesleyan University Press, Conn., 1963)

This book was originally written in French according to the ancient texts and monuments of India.

5. *THE PATH OF THE BUDDHA,* edited by Kenneth Morgan (Ronald Press Co., New York, 1957)

This is the best introductory book on Buddhism with contributions by contemporary Buddhists from various countries. It presents the life and teachings of the Buddha, the spread and development of Buddhism over 2500 years; the attitudes, beliefs, and practices of Buddhists today.

6. *BUDDHISM,* by Christmas Humphreys (A Pelican Book, London, 1952)

The President of the London Buddhist Society describes the history, development and present-day teaching of the various schools of Buddhism.

7. *BUDDHISM, ITS ESSENCE AND DEVELOPMENT,* by Edward Conze (Bruno Cassirer, Oxford, 1953 reprint)

The author gives a general survey of the whole range of Buddhist thought from an objective point of view.

8. *THE BUDDHA'S PHILOSOPHY,* by G. F. Allen (George Allen and Unwin, London, 1953)

The author interprets the most important Buddhist terminologies found in the Pali scriptures.

9. *THE HISTORY OF BUDDHIST THOUGHT*, by Edward Thomas (Routledge & Kegan Paul, London, 1953)
   A well known British scholar traces the historical development of Buddhist thought.
10. *BUDDHISM*, by Richard Gard (George Braziler, New York, 1961)
    Basic Buddhist terminologies are aptly interpreted in this book.

2. BUDDHIST TEXTS IN TRANSLATION

1. *BUDDHISM, A RELIGION OF INFINITE COMPASSIONATE BUDDHA*, by Clarence Hamilton (The Library of Religion, New York, 1952)
   This book contains a comprehensive collection of passages from the main scriptures of both Theravada and Mahayana Buddhism.
2. *THE TEACHINGS OF THE COMPASSIONATE BUDDHA*, by E. A. Burt (Mentor Pocket Book, New York, 1955)
   An elaborate translation of the scriptures of both Theravada and Mahayana Buddhism.
3. *BUDDHISM IN TRANSLATION*, by Henry Warren (Harvard University Press, Cambridge, 1953 reprint)
   This is one of the classic books on Buddhism.
4. *BUDDHIST TEXTS THROUGH THE AGES*, by Conze, Horner, Snellgrove and Waley (Philosophical Library, New York, 1954)

This anthology includes translations from the original Pali, Sanskrit, Chinese, Tibetan, Japanese and Apabhramsa texts.

The whole range of Buddhist thought is well represented in this book.

5. *SOME SAYINGS OF THE BUDDHA,* by F. L. Woodward (Oxford University Press, London, 1960 reprint)

This is a collection of the Buddha's teaching based on the Theravada scriptures.

6. *THE WISDOM OF BUDDHISM,* edited by Christmas Humphreys (Random House, New York, 1961)

This is a new anthology of Buddhist writings found in various Buddhist countries.

7. *THE TEACHING OF BUDDHA,* edited by the Buddhist Promoting Foundation (Tokyo, 1968)

This is a good summary of Buddhist teachings found in the Mahayana scriptures.

8. *THE BUDDHIST TRADITION,* edited by William de Bary and others (Modern Library Edition, New York, 1969)

A well-balanced translation of various writings found in Buddhist tradition in India, China, and Japan.

3. BUDDHISM AND OTHER RELIGIONS

1. *THE RELIGION OF MAN,* by Huston Smith (A Mentor Book, New York, 1958)

The author presents the characteristics of world religions in a sympathetic way.

2. *BUDDHISM AND CHRISTIANITY*, by Winston L. King (George Allen and Unwin Ltd. London, 1963)

   A Christian interpretation of Buddhism, Islam and Christianity is presented in this book.

3. *HINDUISM AND BUDDHISM*, by Ananda K. Coomaraswamy (The Philosophical Library, New York)

   The author describes the difference between the traditional religion of India and the universal religion of Buddhism.

4. *EAST ASIA: THE GREAT TRADITION*, by Edwin O. Reischauer and John K. Fairbank (Houghton Mifflin Co., Boston, 1960)

   The historians trace the sources of East Asian tradition in an objective way.

5. *WAYS OF THINKING OF EASTERN PEOPLES*, by Hajime Nakamura (East-West Center Press, Hawaii, 1964)

   The author characterizes the nature of Indian, Chinese, Tibetan, and Japanese peoples with reference to the written materials.

6. *A COMPARATIVE STUDY OF BUDDHISM AND CHRISTIANITY*, by Fumio Masutani (Young East Assn., Tokyo, 1957)

   The author points out the characteristics of Buddhism and Christianity.

7. *RELIGIONS OF THE EAST*, by Joseph M.

Kitagawa (The Westminster Press, Philadelphia, 1960)

An objective survey on the contemporary religions of the East.

4. JAPANESE BUDDHISM IN GENERAL

1. *JAPANESE BUDDHISM,* by Charles Eliot (Barnes & Noble, New York, 1959 reprint)
This is one of classic books on the history of Japanese Buddhism.

2. *OUTLINE OF MAHAYANA BUDDHISM,* by Daisetz Suzuki (Schoken Books Inc., New York, 1963 reprint)
One of his early works on the origin and development of Mahayana Buddhism.

3. *MAHAYANA BUDDHISM,* by Beatrice Suzuki (The Macmillan Company, New York, 1969 reprint)
This book gives a good summary of the teachings of Mahayana Buddhism.

4. *A GUIDE TO BUDDHISM,* by Shoyu Hanayama Ed., (The International Buddhist Exchange Center, Yokohama, 1970)
This book introduces most of the tenets of Japanese Buddhism.

5. *THE ESSENCE OF BUDDHISM,* by Daisetz Suzuki (London Buddhist Society, London, 1957 reprint)
Though this is a very short book, it conveys the

nature and flavor of Japanese Buddhist teaching.

6. *A HISTORY OF JAPANESE BUDDHISM,* by Shinsho Hanayama (The Buddhist Promoting Foundation, Tokyo, 1966)
The historical survey of Japanese Buddhism down to the present age.

7. *JAPANESE BUDDHISM,* by Shoko Watanabe (Kokusai Bunka Shinkokai, Tokyo, 1964)
A critical appraisal of Japanese Buddhism is reproduced from the Japanese original book.

8. *ESSENTIALS OF BUDDHIST PHILOSOPHY,* by Junjiro Takakusu (The Office Appliance Co., Hawaii, 1954)
The author presents the different tenets of Buddhist philosophy in Japanese Buddhist denominations.

5. DIFFERENT TYPES OF JAPANESE BUDDHISM

1. *ANCIENT BUDDHISM IN JAPAN,* by M. W. de Visser (E. J. Brill, Leiden, 1935, 2 volumes)
This is a scholarly work on the early history of Japanese Buddhism.

2. *ENNIN'S TRAVELS IN T'ANG CHINA* and *ENNIN'S DIARY,* by Edwin O. Reischauer (Ronald Press, New York, 1955 2 volumes)
This is a lucid translation and interpretation

of Ennin, the Japanese Tendai priest who studied Buddhism in medieval China.

3. *MUDRA,* by E. Dale Saunders (Pantheon Books, New York, 1960)

   This book is a study of symbolic gestures in Japanese Buddhist scriptures, particularly in Shingon Buddhism.

4. *HONEN, THE BUDDHIST SAINT, HIS LIFE AND TEACHING,* by H. H. Coats and R. Ishizuka (Sekai Seiten Kankokai, Kyoto, 1949 reprint)

   This is the translation of the authorized biography of Honen, the founder of the Jodo denomination.

5. *SHIN BUDDHISM,* by Daisetz T. Suzuki (Harper & Row, Publishers, New York, 1970)

   It is the comprehensive book on Japan's major religious contribution to the West.

6. *SHINRAN'S GOSPEL OF PURE GRACE,* by Alfred Bloom (The University of Arizona Press, Eugene, 1965)

   A historical survey on the teaching of Shinran, the founder of Shin Buddhism.

7. *JODO SHINSHU,* by Shuken Inaba and Issai Funabashi (Otani University Press, Kyoto, 1961)

   This is an introductory book on Shin Buddhism for the general reader.

8. *AN INTRODUCTION TO SHIN BUDDHISM,* by Kosho Yamamoto (Karin Bunko,

Yamaguchi, 1963)

This is a fair introduction to Shin Buddhism by the author who translated a number of Buddhist scriptures and writings.

9. *BUDDHIST HANDBOOK FOR SHIN-SHU FOLLOWERS,* by Shoyu Hanayama (Hokuseido Press, Tokyo, 1969)

10. *PERFECT FREEDOM IN BUDDHISM,* translated by Shinji Takuwa (The Hokuseido Press, Tokyo, 1968)

An exposition of the words of Shinran with reference to the problems in the contemporary age.

11. *BUDDHISM AND ZEN,* by Senzaki and McCandless (The Wisdom Library, New York, 1953)

This is a concise book on Zen in its relationship to Buddhism.

12. *ZEN BUDDHISM,* by Daisetz Suzuki (A Doubleday Anchor Book, New York, 1956)

This selection of essays, which appeared in his earlier books, expounds Zen as a way of life.

13. *THE WAY OF ZEN,* by Alan Watts (Pantheon, New York, 1949)

An Englishman interprets Zen as his way of life.

14. *ZEN IN ENGLISH LITERATURE AND ORIENTAL CLASSICS,* by R. H. Blyth (Hokuseido Press, Tokyo, 1942)

This book contains the examples of the Zen spirit in English literature.

15. *ZEN AND AMERICAN THOUGHT,* by Van M. Ames (University of Hawaii Press, Hawaii, 1962)

This book contains his unique interpretation of Zen in terms of American pragmatism.

16. *ANTHOLOGY OF ZEN,* Edited by William Briggs (Grove Press, New York, 1931)

This is the collection of writings by Westerners and Japanese who have understood the Zen spirit.

17. *SOTO APPROACH TO ZEN,* by Reiho Masunaga (Laymen's Buddhist Society, Tokyo, 1958)

The Zen known to the West is the Rinzai interpretation. This short book is a good introduction to the teaching of Dogen, the founder of the Soto denomination of Zen Buddhism.

18. *NICHIREN, THE BUDDHIST PROPHET,* by Masaharu Anesaki (Harvard University Press, Cambridge, 1913)

The author describes the life and teaching of Nichiren, the founder of Nichiren Buddhism.

6. BUDDHISM AND ART

1. *THE LIFE OF THE BUDDHA,* by Silva-Vigier (Phaidon Publishing Inc., London 1955)

Famous masterpieces of Buddhist art show the different ways in which the Buddha's life has been interpreted in the art of India, Ceylon,

Burma, Siam, Indonesia, Central Asia, Afghanistan, China, and Japan.

2. *THE WAY OF THE BUDDHA,* Edited by the Publication Division, Government of India, (New Delhi, 1958)

This book tells the story of the Buddha's life and teaching in photographs of the Buddhist art of five different countries.

3. *ART OF FAR LANDS,* by W. Forman (Spring Books, London, 1953)

Many representative Buddhist works of art are well presented in this book.

4. *2000 YEARS OF JAPANESE ART,* by Yukio Yashiro (Harry N. Abrams, Inc., New York, 1958)

This beautiful book is the best guide to Japanese Buddhist art.

5. *JAPANESE TEMPLES AND TEA HOUSES,* by Warner Blaser (F. W. Dodge Corporation, New York, 1953)

This book gives a general survey of traditional Japanese architecture.

6. *MASTERPIECES OF JAPANESE SCULPTURE,* Edited by Edward Kidder (Charles Tuttle Co., Tokyo, 1961)

7. *MASTERWORKS OF JAPANESE ART,* Edited by Charles S. Terry (Charles Tuttle Co., Tokyo, 1960)

This is an excellent work which gives us further

impetus to appreciate the beauty of Japanese Buddhist art.

8. *THE BOOK OF TEA,* by Kakuzo Okakura (Charles Tuttle Co., Tokyo, 1958 reprint)
   The simplicity and serenity of the tea-ceremony, which is an outgrowth of Zen, is described in this beautifully bound book.

9. *ZEN IN THE ART OF ARCHERY,* by Eugene Harrigel (Routledge & Kegan Paul, London, 1957)
   The author learns the way of Zen through his training in Japanese archery.

7. BUDDHISM IN CONTEMPORARY AGE

1. *LIVING BUDDHISM IN JAPAN,* Edited by Yoshiro Tamura (International Institute for the Study of Religions, Tokyo, 1960)
   This is a summary of discussion by the leading Japanese Buddhists.

2. *BUDDHISM OR COMMUNISM,* by Ernst Benz (Doubleday & Co., New York, 1965)
   It deals with the political and social ethics of Buddhism, written by a Christian theologian.

3. *THE NEW FACE OF BUDDHA,* by Jerrold Schecter (John Weatherhill, Tokyo, 1967)
   Although it is a journalistic simplification, this book contains some fine descriptions of modern Buddhist movements in Asia.

4. *BUDDHISM IN HAWAII,* by Louise H. Hunter (University of Hawaii Press, 1971)

A comprehensive sketch of Buddhist missionary
work in Hawaii in the past and present.

8. BIBLIOGRAPHIES

   *1. A BIBLIOGRAPHY ON JAPANESE BUD-
   DHISM,* Edited by Shojun Bando and others
   (Cultural Interchange Institute for Buddhists,
   Tokyo, 1958)

   2. BIBLIOGRAPHY ON BUDDHISM, by Shinsho Hanayama (The Hokuseido Press, Tokyo,
   1961)

   *3. A READER'S GUIDE TO THE GREAT
   RELIGIONS,* Edited by Charles J. Adams
   (The Free Press, New York, 1965)

INDEX: GLOSSARY

TITLE INDEX